EYEWITNESS

WONDERS OF THE WORLD

Palmato gecko

Copper statue of a Chinese dragon

Hopi kachina doll carved out of wood

Coral islands, Great Barrier Reef, Australia

Geode lined with quartz crystals

Reconstructed skull of *Paranthropus boisei*

Burj Khalifa, Dubai, UAE

Taj Mahal, Agra, India

EYEWITNESS

WONDERS OF THE WORLD

WRITTEN BY
TOM JACKSON

The pyramids of Giza, Egypt

Crown-of-thorns
starfish

Penguin
Random
House

Andean flamingos

REVISED EDITION

DK DELHI

Senior Editor Sreshtha Bhattacharya
Senior Art Editor Vikas Chauhan
Editor Bipasha Roy **Art Editors** Noopur Dalal, Aparajita Sen
Assistant Editor Mrinal Pant **Assistant Art Editor** Anastasia Baliyan
DTP Designers Harish Aggarwal, Pawan Kumar, Vikram Singh
Picture Researcher Vishal Ghavri
Managing Editor Kingshuk Ghoshal **Managing Art Editor** Govind Mittal
Jacket Designer Gayatri Menon **Senior Jackets Coordinator** Priyanka Sharma Saddi

DK LONDON

Editor Kelsie Besaw **Art Editor** Chrissy Barnard
Senior US Editor Megan Douglass **US Executive Editor** Lori Cates Hand
Managing Editor Francesca Baines **Managing Art Editor** Philip Letsu
Production Editor Jacqueline Street-Elkayam
Senior Production Controller Jude Crozier
Jacket Design Development Manager Sophia MTT
Publisher Andrew Macintyre
Associate Publishing Director Liz Wheeler
Art Director Karen Self
Publishing Director Jonathan Metcalf

Consultant Peter Chrisp

FIRST EDITION

DK DELHI

Editorial team Shatarupa Chaudhuri, Bharti Bedi,
Ishani Nandi, Priyaneet Singh, Suneha Dutta
Design team Nishesh Batnagar, Amit Varma, Deep Shikha Walia,
Isha Nagar, Nidhi Mehra, Shreya Sadhan
DTP design team Harish Aggarwal, Jagtar Singh, Pawan Kumar
Managing Editor Alka Thakur **Managing Art Editor** Romi Chakraborty
Senior Picture Researcher Sumedha Chopra
Jacket Designers Dhirendra Singh, Suhita Dharamjit

DK LONDON

Editor Ashwin Khurana **Senior Art Editor** Rachael Grady
Jacket Editor Maud Whatley **Jacket Designer** Laura Brim
Jacket Design Development Manager Sophia MTT
Senior Pre-producer Luca Frassinetti **Senior Producer** Charlotte Cade
Managing Editor Gareth Jones **Managing Art Editor** Philip Letsu
Publisher Andrew Macintyre
Associate Publishing Director Liz Wheeler
Art Director Phil Ormerod
Publishing Director Jonathan Metcalf

Consultants John Woodward, Philip Parker

This Eyewitness ® Book has been conceived by
Dorling Kindersley Limited and Editions Gallimard

This American edition, 2022
First American edition, 2014
Dorling Kindersley Limited
Published in the Unites States by DK Publishing
1745 Broadway, 20th Floor, New York, NY 10019

A catalog record for this book
is available from the Library of Congress.
ISBN 978-0-7440-6256-4 (Paperback)
ISBN 978-0-7440-6257-1 (ALB)

DK books are available at special discount when
purchased in bulk for sales promotion,
premiums, fund-raising, or educational use.
For details, contact: DK Publishing Special Markets,
1745 Broadway, 20th Floor, New York, NY 10019
SpecialSales@dk.com

Printed and bound in China

For the curious
www.dk.com

Statue of
Athena

Gold image
of Inti

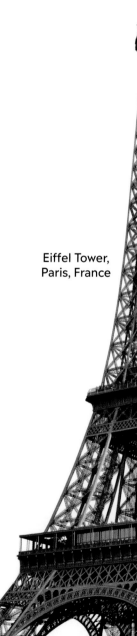

Eiffel Tower,
Paris, France

MIX
Paper | Supporting
responsible forestry
FSC™ C018179

This book was made with Forest Stewardship
Council™ certified paper—one small step in
DK's commitment to a sustainable future.
For more information go to
www.dk.com/our-green-pledge

Contents

DISCLAIMER

First Nations Australian readers are warned that this publication may contain images of deceased persons.

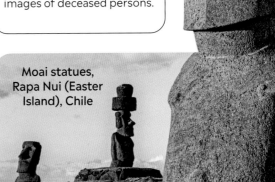

Moai statues, Rapa Nui (Easter Island), Chile

Mount
Everest

The highest place on Earth, the summit (or peak) of Mount Everest rises 29,029 ft (8,848 m) above sea level. The climb to the top—a patch of rock and snow, no bigger than a double bed—is long and dangerous. So far, more than 5,000 climbers have succeeded in reaching the summit.

Everest lies between Nepal and China, and the border runs across the very top of the mountain.

Scaling the peak

In 1953, New Zealander Edmund Hillary (left) and Nepalese Sherpa Tenzing Norgay (right), became the first recorded people to reach the top of Mount Everest. They carried extra oxygen in canisters to help them breathe as they went up.

The Himalayas

The world's highest mountain range, the Himalayas are about 10 million years old. Formed by gradual movements in the Earth's crust, the Himalayas are, in fact, still rising.

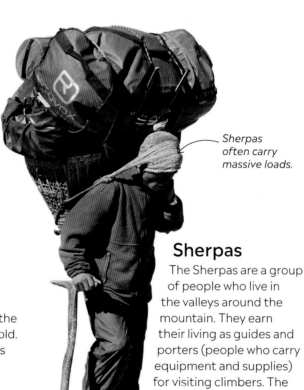

Sherpas often carry massive loads.

Sherpas

The Sherpas are a group of people who live in the valleys around the mountain. They earn their living as guides and porters (people who carry equipment and supplies) for visiting climbers. The world-famous Tenzing Norgay was a Sherpa.

There is a permanent cover of snow at higher altitudes.

Tough terrain

The air at the top of Mount Everest contains only a third of the oxygen it has at ground level. Winds blow at up to 112 mph (180 kph) and temperatures can drop to −80°F (−62°C). Rescue helicopters cannot risk flying at such high altitudes, so injured climbers have to be carried down to safety.

The Nepali name for Mount Everest is Sagarmatha ("The head of Earth touching the sky").

Prayer flags at Rongbuk Monastery

Highest monastery

Located halfway up the northern side of the mountain, Rongbuk Monastery is the world's highest monastery at 16,340 ft (4,980 m). According to Tibetan Buddhist beliefs, the goddess Miyolangsangma lives at the top of the mountain. Many climbers seek her blessing before starting their expedition.

Glimpses of the past

The limestone that forms the top part of Mount Everest contains fossilized seashells and remains of sea animals. The fossils show that the rock—now the highest point on Earth—formed at the bottom of the ocean around 450 million years ago.

Ammonite shell fossil

Art from trash

The long trail leading up to Mount Everest is littered with garbage left behind by careless climbers. In 2012, 1.5 tons of litter was collected, some of which was made into art—including this turtle.

Tin can used to make the turtle's head

Gas tank forms the back.

👁 EYEWITNESS

Junko Tabei
Japanese mountaineer Junko Tabei was the first woman to climb Mount Everest. On the way up, she was buried by an avalanche (a huge amount of snow and rock moving quickly down a mountain). But she did not give up, and reached the top of the mountain on May 19, 1970.

Sandstone carved into a turtle-like shape

Alien landscape

Mount Roraima is mostly made of hard sandstone that has been worn away by daily rainfall and constant winds over millions of years. These harsh conditions can create unusual rock formations, such as the "turtle rock" (above).

Mount Roraima

A 2-billion-year-old flat-topped mountain, Mount Roraima is in the middle of the South American grasslands. "Roraima" means "the great blue-green" in the language of the Pemon people, who have lived here for thousands of years. People did not begin exploring the top of the mountain until it was first climbed in 1884 by a British expedition.

Mount Roraima stands where the borders of Venezuela, Brazil, and Guyana meet in South America.

Tabletop mountain

The Pemon people use the word *tepui* (meaning "house of the gods") to refer to the region's tabletop mountains, which they see as sacred places. At 9,219 ft (2,810 m), Mount Roraima is the highest *tepui* in the area. Heavy rainfall on the mountain's surface flows over its 1,312-ft- (400-m-) steep cliff faces, creating some of the highest waterfalls on Earth.

Predator plants

There is very little soil on top of Mount Roraima. To survive in a place without the essential nutrients found in soil, some native plants, such as this sundew, trap insects for food. Bright drops of a sticky liquid at the ends of the plant's tendrils attract and trap mosquitoes and other bugs. After the plant catches the insect, its leaves close around the prey and digest it.

Sticky liquid on a sundew's spiky leaves traps insects.

Crystal valley

The Valley of Crystals is a small water channel carved into the top of the mountain. Over time, the water has worn away the sandstone surface, exposing the pinkish white quartz beneath. As a result, quartz crystals now line the valley floor like a bed of jewels.

Black skin helps this toad hide among dark rocks.

Roraima bush toad

The Roraima bush toad is found only on Mount Roraima. The species has been cut off from the world for a long time—its closest relative lives in Africa. This proves that the mountain was formed millions of years ago, when Africa and South America were still joined together.

THE LOST WORLD

A RIPPING TALE GUARDIAN

ARTHUR CONAN DOYLE

The lost world

The majestic, mystical Mount Roraima was the inspiration for Arthur Conan Doyle's novel *The Lost World*. Published in 1912, the book tells the story of a group of explorers who climb onto a high, vast plateau hidden by the clouds. Here, they find a land inhabited by dinosaurs and other prehistoric creatures.

👁 EYEWITNESS

Edward Jameson

In 2019, Edward Jameson, who belongs to the Akawaio people of Guyana, became one of the first Indigenous people to climb to the top of Mount Roraima when he scaled its summit with fellow climber Troy Henry. He works as a guide for tourists visiting the mountain.

Mount Fuji is in the southeast of Honshu, Japan's largest island.

Mount Fuji

The highest peak in Japan, Mount Fuji is so large that it can be seen from the city of Tokyo 60 miles (100 km) away. Noted for its great beauty, Mount Fuji is held sacred by the Shinto religion. Although this active volcano last erupted in 1707, scientists believe it will erupt again.

Fire festival

Each summer, the people of Yoshida, a town at the foot of Mount Fuji, hold a fire festival called Yoshida-no-Himatsuri. They light bamboo torches to honor Konohana-sakuya Hime, the Shinto goddess of Mount Fuji. The tradition is thought to keep climbers safe, and also marks the end of the climbing season.

BORN FROM THE ASHES

Crater allows lava and gases to escape from underground.

Layers of ash and lava

Underground magma chamber

Mount Fuji is a stratovolcano—a cone-shaped volcano formed by layers of lava and volcanic ash. The lava comes from a magma (molten rock) chamber that lies beneath Mount Fuji where three tectonic plates (large, moving pieces of Earth's outer layer) meet.

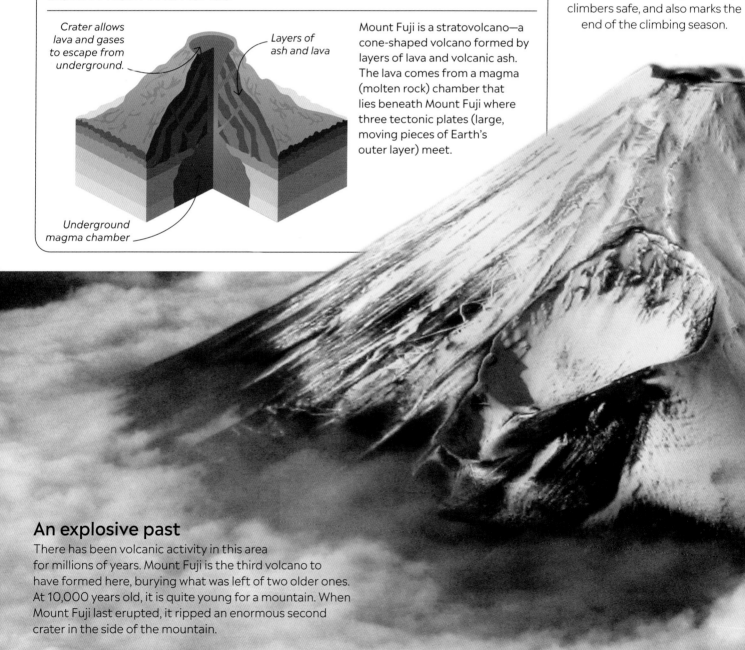

An explosive past

There has been volcanic activity in this area for millions of years. Mount Fuji is the third volcano to have formed here, burying what was left of two older ones. At 10,000 years old, it is quite young for a mountain. When Mount Fuji last erupted, it ripped an enormous second crater in the side of the mountain.

Shrines

There are thousands of Shinto shrines in Japan, where people go to worship kami, the gods and spirits of nature such as mountains. There are many shrines around the base of Mount Fuji, including Fujisan Hongu Sengen Taisha.

Cherry blossoms

The cherry blossom is the symbol of Konohana-sakuya Hime, who is also the goddess of all delicate earthly life. Many Japanese families celebrate spring by having a picnic under cherry trees—a tradition known as *hanami*.

Natural beauty

Japanese artist Katsushika Hokusai portrayed Mount Fuji in a collection of woodblock prints called *36 Views of Mount Fuji*.

Fuji from Kanaya on the Tokaido road, by Katsushika Hokusai

To the top

In summer, tens of thousands of people climb to the peak at 12,389 ft (3,776 m). Visitors travel half the way by bus, then walk to the top—a journey of about 4 hours. Many climb at night so they can watch the sunrise from the peak.

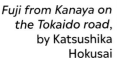

Old Faithful

The most famous geyser in the world, Old Faithful, is so called because it is both regular and predictable. It is one of 200 geysers in Yellowstone National Park, which also features hot springs, boiling mud pools, and fumaroles (outlets that let out steam and other gases).

Old Faithful is located in Yellowstone National Park in Wyoming.

WHAT IS A GEYSER?

A geyser is a spring that releases hot water and steam from the ground. Beneath Old Faithful is a deep underground reservoir, containing boiling water heated to almost 400°F (200°C) by magma (molten rock). This water regularly surges to the surface through a crack leading to the geyser, and erupts as a fountain.

Spray of water and steam from the geyser

Hot spring

Groundwater seeps down through rocks

The water is heated when it comes in contact with hot rocks.

Boiling water rises to surface

Molten rock, or magma

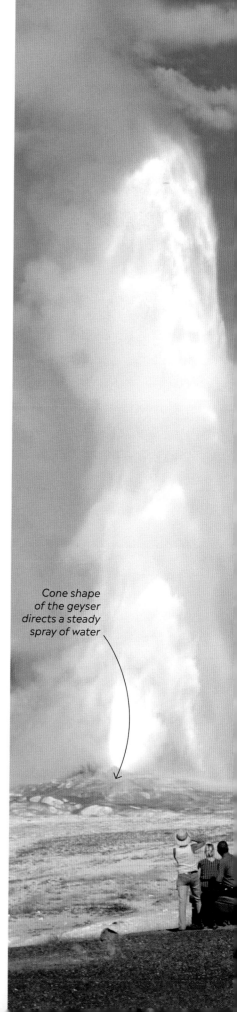

Cone shape of the geyser directs a steady spray of water

Old Faithful Inn

Yellowstone National Park receives more than 3 million visitors a year. Most tour the park by bus or car. However, some of the best views of Old Faithful are from a nearby hotel, which has been hosting tourists for more than a century.

Old-fashioned bus on a park tour

Right on time!

Old Faithful erupts every 91 minutes, on average, and the displays generally last 2–3 minutes during which up to 8,454 gallons (32,000 liters) of water is squirted into the sky. However, Old Faithful has slowed down since its discovery in 1870, when it used to erupt every 65 minutes. The longer interval may be the result of a change in the underground water levels due to earthquakes in the region.

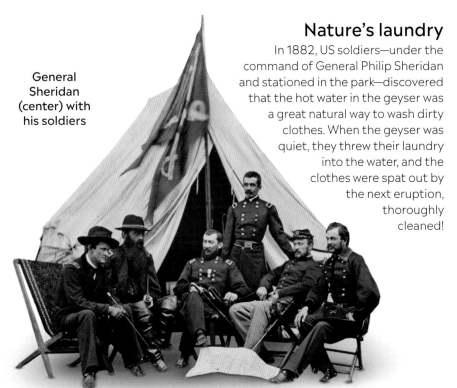

General Sheridan (center) with his soldiers

Nature's laundry

In 1882, US soldiers—under the command of General Philip Sheridan and stationed in the park—discovered that the hot water in the geyser was a great natural way to wash dirty clothes. When the geyser was quiet, they threw their laundry into the water, and the clothes were spat out by the next eruption, thoroughly cleaned!

First national park

In 1872, Yellowstone became the first national park in the world. The name Yellowstone comes from the Minnetaree name for the main river in the park, *Mi tse a-da-zi* (Yellowstone River), meaning "rock yellow."

Giant Prismatic Spring

The Giant Prismatic Spring in Yellowstone National Park is the largest hot spring in the United States. The bright bands of color in the spring are produced by bacteria that grow in hot water.

The **Dead Sea**

Nestled in the mountains between Israel and Jordan, the Dead Sea is 31 miles (50 km) long and 9 miles (15 km) wide. The Dead Sea is, in fact, a lake—one of the saltiest on Earth. Its surface lies 1,400 ft (427 m) below sea level, making its shoreline the lowest patch of dry land on Earth.

The Dead Sea lies between Israel, Jordan, and Palestine.

Salt content

Water flows into the Dead Sea from the Jordan River. The water gets trapped in the lake and evaporates in the fierce heat of the sun, leaving salt crystals behind on the shore.

The paler sediments here show that the water level was once much higher.

Water here is almost 10 times saltier than that of the ocean.

Floating away
The lake's water is very dense because it contains so much salt. It is much denser than the human body, allowing swimmers to float around effortlessly on the surface.

Swimmers need to be careful to keep the salty, stinging water out of their eyes.

Asphalt

The Dead Sea releases a material called asphalt—an oily, solid form of petroleum—through cracks in its seabed. Lumps of asphalt can be seen floating on the lake's surface.

The Dead Sea refinery at Sedom, Israel, harvests bromine from the water.

Mineral wealth

The southern part of the lake contains shallow pools, where the water evaporates, leaving behind minerals such as bromine. This unusual red-brown liquid is used in fire-retardants, which stop things from burning.

Is the Dead Sea dying?

Much of the ground around the lake is drying out and collapsing into sinkholes (above)—holes that can open up suddenly as a result of erosion. The Dead Sea is currently shrinking at the rate of about 39 in (1 m) per year.

Ancient secrets

The Dead Sea Scrolls are 972 sacred Jewish manuscripts, found at Qumrān in the West Bank between 1946 and 1947. Written between 250 BCE and 70 CE, the scrolls are thought to have belonged to a local religious community. These were hidden in caves, stored inside pottery jars, for safekeeping.

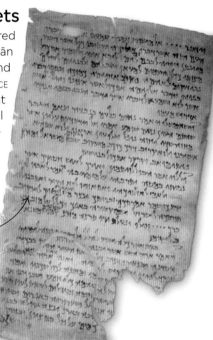

Ink made from soot on goatskin parchment

The Dead Sea is called
Al-Bar Al-Mayyit
("Sea of Death") in Arabic.

Dead Sea mud helps cleanse the skin.

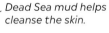

Health benefits

Rich in minerals, the Dead Sea's water and mud are believed to ease pain in muscles and joints. Breathing the air above the lake is also thought to have health benefits, as it is free of pollen and other particles that cause allergies such as hay fever.

👁 EYEWITNESS

Muhammad edh-Dibh

At the age of 15, this Bedouin goatherd discovered the Dead Sea Scrolls in the 1940s. While searching for a missing goat, Muhammad edh-Dibh threw some stones into a cave, and heard the sound of breaking pottery from the jars in which the scrolls were stored. This photograph shows him standing outside the cave. Later, more pots with scrolls were found in neighboring caves.

The Grand Canyon is in a high desert region of northern Arizona.

The Grand Canyon

The spectacular Grand Canyon was cut into the desert rocks by the Colorado River. The canyon is so wide that an entire city could fit between its rims, and so deep that the world's tallest building could fit inside it twice over.

Mule delivery along a canyon trail

Mule mail

There are no roads in the Grand Canyon, just steep, rocky tracks. Mules are used for transportation and for carrying mail. Supai, a village deep inside the canyon, is the only place in the US where the mail still arrives by mule.

Indigenous peoples

The Grand Canyon has been home to people for thousands of years. But since 1540, when the Spanish conqueror Garcia Lopez de Cardenas visited the canyon, outsiders, including industrialists, scientists, and the US government, have claimed the place as their own. Indigenous peoples such as the Hopi and Havasupai still live in the area, and are reclaiming their ancestral land.

Hopi kachina doll carved out of wood

Colorado River

The canyon

A canyon is a deep valley with steep sides, usually with a river flowing through it. Created over 3 million years, the Grand Canyon was formed when the land around it was pushed upward, and the Colorado River cut through many layers of rock. It is 277 miles (446 km) long, up to 18 miles (29 km) wide, and about 1 mile (1.6 km) deep.

About 120 people can stand on the Skywalk at a time.

Skywalk

Shaped like a horseshoe, with a see-through floor, the Skywalk bridge allows tourists to stand 4,000 ft (1,220 m) above the Colorado River. More than 4 million tourists visit the canyon every year. While most come to enjoy the view, some hike to the bottom or take thrilling helicopter rides.

The Skywalk extends out 70 ft (21 m) from the canyon wall.

👁 EYEWITNESS

Dianna Sue WhiteDove Uqualla
A leader of the Havasupai Nation, Dianna Sue WhiteDove Uqualla leads traditional ceremonies and welcomes visitors to the Grand Canyon, teaching them Havasupai customs. She has campaigned to stop uranium mining around the canyon, which pollutes the water there.

Risk takers

In 2013, American acrobat Nik Wallenda walked 1,400 ft (427 m) on a high wire 1,500 ft (457 m) above the canyon floor. In 1999, American stunt performer Robbie Knievel jumped across the canyon on a motorcycle.

Animals and plants

The Grand Canyon is home to several plants and animals that exist only there. The Kaibab squirrel lives mainly in the canyon's northern forests. Commonly found animals, such as mule deer and bighorn sheep, live mainly on the south side of the canyon.

Broad, feathery tail

Kata Tjuta

Kata Tjuta is a cluster of 36 domes of rock, the highest of which is 656 ft (200 m) taller than Uluru. On the surface, Kata Tjuta lies about 16 miles (25 km) from Uluru, but the two rock formations are linked underground.

Uluru

Uluru is sacred to Australia's First Nations peoples. One of the world's largest rocks, it has a circumference of 5.8 miles (9.4 km) and is 1,142 ft (348 m) tall at its highest point. Every day, hundreds of tourists visit Uluru to tour around the base and to view the First Nations rock art sites in the region.

Uluru lies near the center of Australia, close to the city of Alice Springs.

The rock

Made up of a sandstone called arkose, Uluru gets its red color from iron-rich minerals in the rock. As the angle of the sun changes through the day, the rock can look red, orange, yellow, or gray.

Uluru turns a deep orange-yellow at sunrise and sunset.

CONCEALED CONNECTIONS

Uluru and Kata Tjuta are the two ends of a thick rock layer. At ground level, Uluru rises as a huge single dome, whereas the pebble-filled rock of Kata Tjuta has been worn away into several sections.

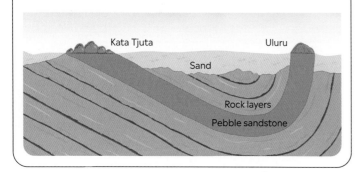

Kata Tjuta

Uluru

Sand

Rock layers

Pebble sandstone

Sacred land

The Anangu people have lived in the Uluru region for thousands of years. First Nations Australian spirituality is deeply tied to the land, and so Indigenous peoples work hard to protect and honor it. Tourists are not allowed to visit certain sacred sites.

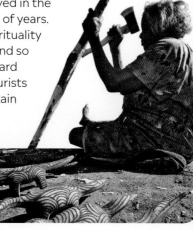

Woman from the Anangu community preparing wood for carving artifacts

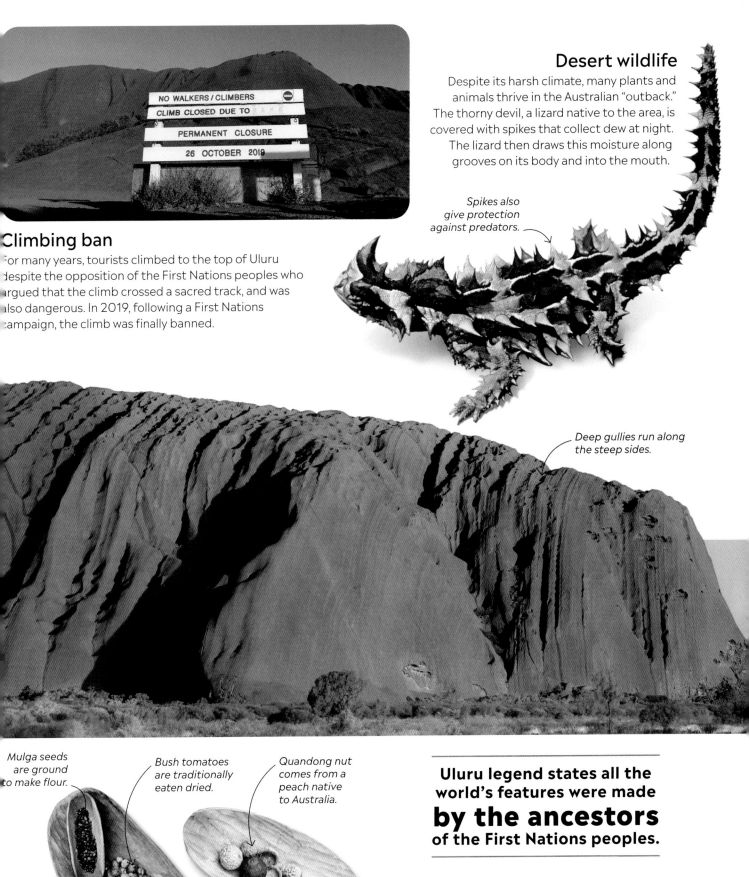

Desert wildlife

Despite its harsh climate, many plants and animals thrive in the Australian "outback." The thorny devil, a lizard native to the area, is covered with spikes that collect dew at night. The lizard then draws this moisture along grooves on its body and into the mouth.

Spikes also give protection against predators.

Climbing ban

For many years, tourists climbed to the top of Uluru despite the opposition of the First Nations peoples who argued that the climb crossed a sacred track, and was also dangerous. In 2019, following a First Nations campaign, the climb was finally banned.

NO WALKERS / CLIMBERS
CLIMB CLOSED DUE TO
PERMANENT CLOSURE
26 OCTOBER 2019

Deep gullies run along the steep sides.

Mulga seeds are ground to make flour.

Bush tomatoes are traditionally eaten dried.

Quandong nut comes from a peach native to Australia.

Bush tucker served on carved wooden plates

Uluru legend states all the world's features were made **by the ancestors** of the First Nations peoples.

Bush tucker

Any food native to Australia, and traditionally eaten by the First Nations peoples, is called bush tucker. The name usually refers to fruits and nuts that grow in the dry desert region around Uluru, but also includes meat from local animals, such as kangaroos and lizards. Insects, such as ants and caterpillars, are also often a part of the diet.

The Cave of Crystals is in Chihuahua, a state in northern Mexico.

The Cave of Crystals

The Naica Mine, in Mexico, is famous for its beautiful crystal caves. The most spectacular of these is the Cave of Crystals, which houses the biggest crystals in the world. In 2000, two brothers accidentally discovered this cave while drilling an underground tunnel to look for lead ore.

Crystal palace

The Cave of Crystals is a limestone cavern. Most of its crystals are at least 20 ft (6 m) long, while the largest discovered here so far is twice that size and weighs 55 tons. Only a few scientists are allowed into the cave to study these fragile crystals.

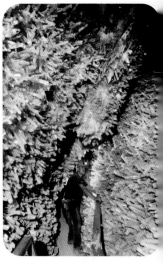

Cave of Swords

Named after its daggerlike crystals, the Cave of Swords was found near the surface of the Naica Mine in 1910. It contains similar but smaller crystals to those found in the Cave of Crystals.

These crystals are soft enough to be scratched with a fingernail.

Scientists wear rubber boots, because they must take care not to damage the soft crystals.

FORMATION OF THE CRYSTALS

Over a period of about half a million years, the Cave of Crystals was flooded with hot water that rose from deep underground. Dissolved minerals in the water crystallized gradually as the water washed through the cave. When miners pumped the water out of the cave to look for lead ore, the crystals stopped growing.

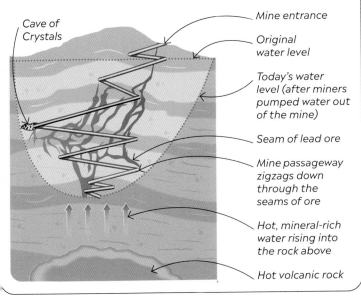

Cave of Crystals

Mine entrance

Original water level

Today's water level (after miners pumped water out of the mine)

Seam of lead ore

Mine passageway zigzags down through the seams of ore

Hot, mineral-rich water rising into the rock above

Hot volcanic rock

A humidity meter is used to measure moisture in the air around the crystals.

Risky business

The temperature in the cave is at least 112°F (44°C). Scientists called crystallographers wear rubber suits containing ice-filled tubes and carry a supply of cooled, dry air to help them breathe. Without this equipment, they would become ill after just 10 minutes.

Giant geode

The Cave of Crystals has been called a giant geode—a mass of crystals that forms in spaces inside rocks. The space gets filled with mineral-rich water, and the minerals slowly turn into crystals.

Geodes, such as this one, usually contain quartz crystals.

Gypsum galore

The crystals found in the Cave of Crystals are made of selenite, a form of the mineral gypsum. Gypsum is very common and occurs in different forms, including desert rose and ram's horn. It is used to make plaster (for building) and drawing chalk.

Desert rose

Ram's horn

Salar de Uyuni

The largest salt flat in the world, Salar de Uyuni stretches across an area of 4,086 sq miles (10,582 sq km)—10 times the size of Los Angeles—and is covered in a 3-ft- (1-m-) thick crust of salt. It is also the world's flattest place, with less than 3 ft (1 m) between its highest and lowest points.

Salar de Uyuni lies on the Altiplano, a high plateau in Bolivia, South America.

The great salt flats

Salar de Uyuni fills a hollow basin surrounded by the Andes Mountains. Rain and flood water gets trapped in the area because there is nowhere for it to flow out. Over time, the water evaporates, leaving behind deposits of salt and other minerals

Viscachas live in large groups known as colonies.

Visual delights

Each year, the monsoon rains flood the salt flat, turning it into a vast pool. The still water creates such perfect reflections that it is difficult to tell where the ground stops and the sky begins.

Life in the desert

Plants cannot survive on the salt flats. However, hardy shrubs and cacti grow on the rocky islands, where they provide food for animals such as the large, rabbitlike rodents called viscachas.

Land-locked islands

The rocky islands, such as Isla Pabellon, rising above the salt are the peaks of ancient volcanoes that were once submerged under a prehistoric lake. With little rainfall and no other major source of water nearby, the lake dried out about 15,000 years ago, exposing the peaks we see today.

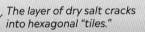

Flock together

Large flocks of flamingos fly to Salar de Uyuni every November and gather by shallow pools to raise their young. The birds lay eggs in nests made from mounds of mud. When the eggs hatch, the adults feed their chicks tiny shrimp that thrive in the salty water.

The layer of dry salt cracks into hexagonal "tiles."

Mineral mine

Salar de Uyuni contains an estimated 10.8 billion tons of salt—27,558 tons of which is mined for use in cooking every year. Miners dig through the solid crust to reach a wet, salty mush called brine. Valuable minerals can be extracted from the brine, including the metal lithium, which is used in rechargeable batteries.

About 70 percent of the world's lithium reserves are found in Salar de Uyuni.

Salt hotels

Visitors can stay in salt hotels, where everything from the walls to furniture is made of blocks of salt. When it rains, the salt mixes with the water and gets washed away, so regular repairs are needed.

The Serengeti

The Serengeti (derived from a local word meaning "the land that goes on forever") is a wide open plain in East Africa. Every year, more than a million animals make a long journey known as the Great Migration, which draws in many tourists. People also go on a safari or visit other attractions such as the Ngorongoro Crater.

The Serengeti covers an area of 12,000 sq miles (30,000 sq km) across the border between Kenya and Tanzania.

As old as time

On the eastern edge of the Serengeti is the Olduvai Gorge. Fossil bones and stone tools found here tell us that hominids—the ancient relatives of humans—lived in the area around 2 million years ago. Two hominid species lived in the gorge—*Paranthropus boisei* and *Homo habilis*.

Zebras eat dry, tough grasses, while the wildebeest eat the soft grasses left behind.

The vast plains

The Serengeti is a savanna—a mixture of grassland and scattered trees—with woods and wetlands. The eastern part gets the least rain and is covered in short grasses. Moving west, the rainfall increases and taller grasses grow there. Farther west, the grassland becomes a thorny woodland, and then a wetland where it meets Lake Victoria (Victoria Nyanza)..

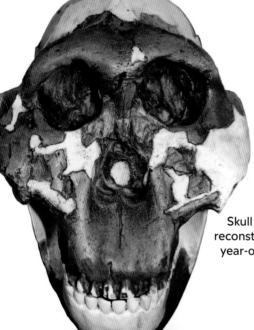

Male wildebeest can have horns up to 32 in (80 cm) long.

Skull of *Paranthropus boisei* reconstructed using 1.75-million-year-old fossil fragments from Olduvai Gorge

Great Migration

Every year, 1.2 million wildebeest make a 500-mile (800-km) journey across the Serengeti. In spring, the wildebeest give birth in the eastern grasslands. By May, the grass begins to run out, and the herds move to the western wetlands. When these wetlands dry up in July, the wildebeest go north. In winter, they head back east, and the cycle begins again. This is the largest mass animal migration left that still takes place on Earth.

Each February around
8,000 wildebeest
calves are born
every day.

Predator alert!
A quarter of the animals making the Great Migration die on the journey. While thousands of them drown as they cross rivers, many of them are killed by predators. Spotted hyenas (right) often hunt in packs to bring down much larger prey.

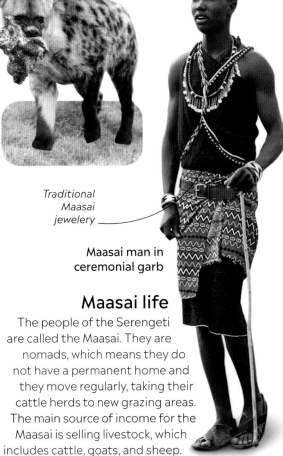

Volcanic neighbors
The 12½-mile- (20-km-) wide Ngorongoro Crater is located in the volcanic mountains along the eastern end of the Serengeti. It is one of the largest volcanic craters in the world. In the rainy season, the crater fills with water, forming Lake Magadi.

Traditional Maasai jewelery

Maasai man in ceremonial garb

Maasai life
The people of the Serengeti are called the Maasai. They are nomads, which means they do not have a permanent home and they move regularly, taking their cattle herds to new grazing areas. The main source of income for the Maasai is selling livestock, which includes cattle, goats, and sheep.

25

The Namib Desert

One of the harshest deserts in the world, the Namib Desert stretches across 1,243 miles (2,000 km). It features some of the world's highest dunes, along with dried-up marshes and a rocky coast. The red sand of the Namib is about 80 million years old, making the desert one of the oldest on Earth.

The Namib Desert is situated along the southwest coast of Africa.

The sun scorches the wood, blackening it.

Against all odds

Unique to this area is the Welwitschia, which can be found near the coast. It grows by trapping moisture from the sea fog in its leaves. It can survive for more than 1,000 years. It has just two leaves, which get shredded by the strong winds.

Leaves grow up to 13 ft (4 m) long.

Dead marsh

Surrounded by massive dunes, Deadvlei (meaning "dead marsh") was once a desert oasis. It was formed when the Tsauchab River flooded the region, creating shallow pools that allowed the camel thorn trees to grow. All that remains today is dry clay and dead tree trunks.

The red dunes

The dunes in the desert's Sossusvlei region are some of the highest in the world. Among the most famous are the Big Daddy (1,066 ft/325 m high) and Dune 7 (1,257 ft/383 m high). The dunes are formed by red, iron-rich sand, and range from orange to red.

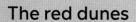

Desert elephants

African elephants can survive in the Namib Desert because they have adapted to its harsh, dry climate. They keep cool by coating themselves with sand, and can go for days without water, surviving on the moisture in their food. Sometimes they make long journeys at night to reach watering holes.

Large feet make it easier to walk on sand.

Drinking in

The palmato gecko can only be found in the Namib Desert. As it has no eyelids, the gecko uses its long tongue to clean its eyes. It also uses its tongue to "drink" condensed fog from its eyes to help it survive in the dry conditions.

Skeleton Coast

The shoreline of the Namib Desert, the Skeleton Coast, is known for its heavy surf and sea fog. It gets its name from the skeletons of sea animals and remains of shipwrecks. Ships lose their way in the thick fog, and are wrecked on the offshore rocks. The local people nicknamed this coast "the land god made in anger."

Shipwreck on the Skeleton Coast

Dune in Sossusvlei at sunset

The Giant
Forest

Some of the world's largest trees grow on the mountain slopes of central California. Standing 6,000 ft (1,829 m) above sea level, the Giant Forest is home to towering giant sequoia trees— the largest living things on Earth.

The Giant Forest is part of the Sequoia National Park in California.

Small beginnings

Each year, the larger sequoias grow up to 11,000 cones, which release around 300,000 seeds. Each seed is only 0.15 in (4 mm) long and has tiny wings.

Colossal trees

The Giant Forest is one of 68 areas of forest in California where giant sequoias grow. These trees can grow to 311 ft (94.8 m) in height and 49,440 cubic ft (1,400 cubic m) in volume, and can live longer than 3,000 years. Five of the largest trees in the world— including the President, a giant sequoia that is around 3,200 years old—are found here.

Human	Giraffe		General Sherman	Lindsey Creek (died in 1905)
6 ft (1.8 m)	18 ft (5.5 m)		274.9 ft (83.8 m)	390 ft (118.9 m)

RECORD BREAKERS

The largest living tree by volume is the giant sequoia General Sherman, with a volume of 52,508 cubic ft (1,487 cubic m). The tallest living tree is Hyperion, a coastal redwood at 379.3 ft (115.6 m). The biggest tree on record was Lindsey Creek, a coastal redwood with a volume of 90,052 cubic ft (2,550 cubic m).

A forest ecologist climbs up to measure the tree's height.

The President, the third largest tree in the world, with a height of 246 ft (75 m) and a volume of 45,167 cubic ft (1,279 cubic m).

Jim Spickler

American canopy scientist Jim Spickler studies the tops of trees. In 2006, he climbed Hyperion, a giant coastal redwood. By dropping a long tape measure from the top, Spickler showed that Hyperion was the world's tallest tree.

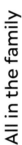

All in the family

Although they are closely related, coastal redwoods in California are much taller than giant sequoias, growing up to 328 ft (100 m). A tunnel cut through a coastal redwood is wide enough to accommodate a car, as seen in the Chandelier Tree in California's Drive-Thru Tree Park.

Safety first

Wildfires can spread quickly in summer. Forest fire teams burn any dead wood and dry leaves before they catch fire in order to protect the wildlife and nearby communities.

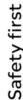

Circle of life

A tree's age can be determined by the number of rings on its trunk. Every season, a tree produces new layers of wood around the trunk. Each layer looks slightly different, which makes it possible to count and study the rings. The rings on this coastal redwood in Muir Woods, California, show it was 1,021 years old.

1930: The tree falls

1908: Muir Woods National Monument established

1776: US Declaration of Independence

1492: Columbus sails to America

1325: The Aztecs begin construction of Tenochtitlán, Mexico

909 CE: The tree is born

Great
Barrier Reef

The Great Barrier Reef runs through the western end of the Coral Sea.

Stretching along the northeastern coast of Australia, the Great Barrier Reef is the world's largest structure made by living organisms. At 1,600 miles (2,600 km) long, it can even be seen from space. However, the reef is increasingly threatened by the effects of global warming.

The reef
Coral reefs are made up of skeletons of corals. Each coral piece is formed from thousands of tiny animals called polyps. Many polyps have hard cases, which they leave behind when they die. New polyps grow on top of these skeletons, and the reef builds up at about 0.39 in (1 cm) a year.

In the shallows
Coral has been growing along the Australian coast for 25 million years, but the current reef is about 7,000 years old. The Great Barrier Reef measures 492 ft (150 m) at its deepest point and consists of around 3,000 individual coral reefs.

Animal life
The reef is home to thousands of marine animals, including six species of turtle, 17 species of sea snake, 1,500 types of fish, and dozens of different kinds of sharks. The moray eel is one of the reef's most ferocious hunters. It hides among the coral until it is time to find its next meal.

A crown-of-thorns starfish has up to 21 arms.

Dangerous pest
The crown-of-thorns starfish eats the soft parts of coral. It turns its stomach inside out to engulf its prey. Hungry swarms of these starfish can kill large parts of the reef, which often take years to recover.

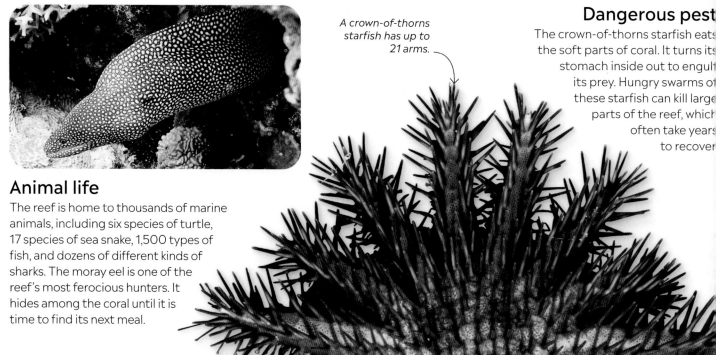

Bright light helps the diver to see the reef's colors.

Underwater video camera

Marine biologists study the marine life and make sure human activities are not damaging the reef.

Making food

Coral polyps use their tentacles to gather food particles, but they also get food from microscopic, plantlike algae that live inside their bodies. These algae produce sugar, which they share with the polyps.

Stony corals release bundles of cells into the water.

Coral spawning

Corals spawn (produce young) by releasing male and female reproductive cells into the water. These combine to form baby corals, which can swim. Once a year, entire colonies of coral spawn at the same time, releasing great clouds of cells into the water at night.

Victoria Falls

Victoria Falls/Mosi-oa-Tunya forms the border between Zambia and Zimbabwe in southern Africa.

Measuring 328 ft (100 m) high and 5,597 ft (1,706 m) wide, Victoria Falls is the world's biggest sheet of falling water. Its African name is Mosi-oa-Tunya, which means "the smoke that thunders" in the Lozi language. From February to May, when the river is at full flow, the waterfall makes a roaring sound and sends up clouds of spray.

The falls

Following the November rains, the Zambezi River pushes enough water to fill an Olympic-size swimming pool over the falls every two seconds. This produces a 1,312-ft- (400-m-) tall cloud of spray. In the dry season, the water level goes down, splitting the falls into four separate torrents.

Extreme sports

The waterfall is a major destination for adventure sports. A majestic railroad bridge close to Victoria Falls/Mosi-oa-Tunya serves as a perfect site for bungee jumping. Thrill seekers can also zip across the water, suspended from a cable between the craggy cliffs, or navigate rafts through the Zambezi River's ferocious rapids.

Haven for wildlife

This region of dry grasslands and bushes does not receive much rainfall, but there is enough spray from the falls for a tiny rainforest to thrive on the surrounding riverbanks. This provides a lush habitat for animals such as hippos, which are not found elsewhere in the area.

Zigzagging river

The Zambezi River zigzags through six river gorges—four of which are shown here. These narrow valleys are carved as running water wears away the rock underneath. Victoria Falls/Mosi-oa-Tunya lies at the top of the first of these gorges.

In the Queen's name

In 1855, Scottish explorer David Livingstone became the first European to view this waterfall. He named it after Queen Victoria of Britain. But now, more and more people are beginning to call the falls by their local name, "Mosi-oa-Tunya."

Devil's Pool

One of the ways to get a good view of Victoria Falls/ Mosi-oa-Tunya is from the top. Local guides take visitors to the Devil's Pool, a safe place right on the edge to sit and watch the water gushing past. The Devil's Pool is only accessible in the dry season, when the current is not too strong.

Lascaux Cave
paintings

In 1940, four teenage boys looking for treasure discovered the Lascaux Cave in France when they followed their pet dog called Robot. Instead of gold and jewels, they found paintings, drawings, and engravings that covered the walls of the cave. These prehistoric pictures have been preserved for more than 16,000 years.

Lascaux Cave is in the Dordogne region of southern France, an area famous for its caves.

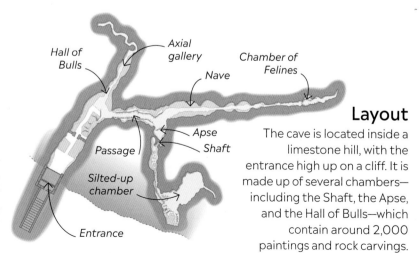

Layout
The cave is located inside a limestone hill, with the entrance high up on a cliff. It is made up of several chambers—including the Shaft, the Apse, and the Hall of Bulls—which contain around 2,000 paintings and rock carvings.

Animal kingdom
Many of the cave paintings feature animals. This picture, known as "The Crossed Bison," is in the Nave. There are also paintings of extinct species, such as the cave hyena and woolly rhinoceros.

Hall of Bulls

The largest paintings are in the Hall of Bulls, which features giant bulls as well as stags and horses. The central bull is 11½ ft (3.5 m) long. The animal on the far left is an unidentified creature with two horns.

The figures were probably created using either manganese dioxide or charcoal.

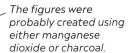

Needle

Harpoon

Saw

Tools of the trade

The Lascaux paintings were created during the last Ice Age. The artists were hunters, who made tools from the bones of deer and other animals.

The wounded man

There is only one picture of a human in the entire cave. In it, a man appears to have been knocked over by the bull to his right. One interpretation is that the little bird below represents his spirit.

Replica cave

The original cave has now been closed to protect the fragile paintings. Visitors can instead go to Lascaux II, a replica cave nearby.

Red color was made from iron oxide.

Wall recreated using a 3D survey of the real cave wall

Pigments used

The cave artists made their pigments from crushed rocks and earth mixed with water or saliva. They painted using a stick, a brush, or their fingers. The colors could also be sprayed on the wall through a hollow bird bone or reed.

Stonehenge

A circle of megaliths (giant stones), Stonehenge is one of the world's most famous Stone Age structures. Its most iconic feature are the trilithons—two large stones with a third laid across the top. The circle was built for ritual purposes, including burials and ceremonies linked with the movements of the sun. At midwinter, people from a wide area of Britain gathered here for feasts and ceremonies.

Stonehenge is located on the Salisbury Plain in southern England, UK.

Sun and moon

Stonehenge is aligned with the midwinter sunset and the midsummer sunrise. Some stones may also be aligned with the rising and setting of the moon.

Three-stone structure known as a trilithon

STAGES OF CONSTRUCTION

Stonehenge was built in stages, and its design changed over time. It began as a big circle of small bluestones, which the builders brought all the way from Wales, 240 miles (385 km) away. Later, bigger sarsen stones, quarried 19 miles (30 km) away, were set up as trilithons.

Outer station stones

1 Bluestone circle (c.3000–2920 BCE)

There were originally 56 bluestones, set up in a big circle (shown as dots) surrounded by a bank and ditches.

2 Trilithons built (c. 2500 BCE)

Five trilithons, surrounded by a trilithon circle, were set up. The bluestones were rearranged in a double circle between them.

3 Inner bluestone oval (c.2200 BCE)

Some of the bluestones were rearranged into an oval inside the central trilithons, leaving an outer single circle of bluestones.

Houses were timber, with thatched roofs

Settlement
The people who built Stonehenge lived nearby, at Durrington Walls, where archaeologists have found post holes from their houses. Animal bones show that great feasts were held here at midwinter.

Burial site
Stonehenge was a burial site. The first post holes for the bluestones held cremated (burned) human bones. Tests on these suggest that the people buried here came from Wales. Later, intact bodies were buried at Stonehenge, along with grave goods such as stone axes and arrowheads.

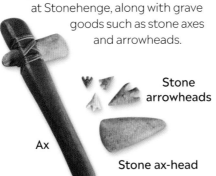
Ax

Stone arrowheads

Stone ax-head

Druids
In the 17th century, scholars who studied Stonehenge suggested that it was a temple built by Druids—Celtic priests who lived in Britain 2,000 years ago. In fact, the monument is much older. Even so, modern-day Druids still gather at Stonehenge for ceremonies at midwinter and midsummer.

Remains of outer circle of sarsen stones

Carhenge
Located in Nebraska, this replica of Stonehenge is made from old cars sprayed with gray paint. Jim Reinders built Carhenge as a memorial to his father, using a total of 38 cars.

Today's site
Stonehenge may have had up to 165 stones when it was built, but many are now missing or have fallen. In the Middle Ages, the monument was used as a source of stones to build nearby churches.

The Nazca Lines

Covered in hundreds of giant patterns, the Nazca desert in Peru is the largest drawing board in the world. The Nazca Lines were created around 1,500 years ago, but lay forgotten until the late 1920s. Without an aircraft, it is impossible to see the designs in full.

The Nazca Lines are in southeastern Peru, about 12½ miles (20 km) from the Pacific Ocean.

Straight lines surround the spider.

Geoglyphs

The Nazca Lines are geoglyphs—patterns on the ground made using rocks, gravel, and soil. One of the many patterns seen here in the desert is that of the Nazca Monkey (left). Other examples of geoglyphs include the 2,000-year-old Paracas Candelabra in northern Peru and stone wheel patterns found in the Arabian Desert.

Drawings on the ground

The Nazca people are thought to have marked the lines using ropes and stakes. They then created the pictures by hand, removing the dark upper rocks to reveal the lighter soil beneath. Here, the tail portion of the 305-ft- (93-m-) long Nazca Hummingbird (right) is visible.

Mysterious lines

Most of the Nazca Lines are spirals, geometric shapes, and straight lines. However, about 70 of them are pictures of animals and plants—including a monkey, a hummingbird, and this 154-ft- (47-m-) long spider. Adding to the mystery, some of these patterns are in the shape of animals not found in this region, such as the monkey.

Some Nazca lines are
30 miles
(48 km) long.

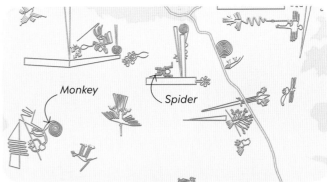

Monkey

Spider

Big pictures

The Nazca Lines cover an area of 100 sq miles (260 sq km). There are around 900 designs, all made between 400 and 650 CE. The largest pictures are almost 1,260 ft (385 m) long. Since this area gets little rain or wind, the lines have remained intact over the centuries.

Mummified remains

The Nazca people were farmers and skilled craftworkers who lived in the fertile river valleys to the north and south of the lines. The dry, desert conditions have preserved many of their bodies as mummies and much of what we know about them comes from their graves.

Well-preserved mummy found in the Chauchilla Cemetery in Nazca, Peru

Animal motifs

Animal shapes were common in the artwork of the Nazca people. This small jug is in the shape of a killer whale, with sharp teeth and two spouts on top for pouring.

Moai statues

The Pacific island of Rapa Nui, or Easter Island, is home to around 900 stone statues, called *moai*. They represent the islanders' ancestors, who were worshipped as gods. Rapa Nui is the most remote inhabited place on Earth. When the first Europeans visited in 1722, the islanders had not had contact with other people for 1,000 years. By 1744, most of the *moai* had been torn down.

Easter Island lies in the Pacific Ocean, 2,175 miles (3,500 km) from the coast of Chile.

Similar proportions

The *moai* were carved using rock from a volcanic crater. All of the statues have similar proportions: the huge head makes up a third of the statue. Each face has a wide chin, a long, pointed nose, and rectangular earlobes.

The Pukao, *or topknot, is cut from a type of volcanic rock called red scoria.*

33 ft (10 m)

6 ft (1.8 m)

Paro compared to a human

Larger than life

Most *moai* are about 13 ft (4 m) high. The tallest one, named Paro, is 33 ft (10 m) tall and weighs 90 tons (82 metric tons).

Ancient script

The islanders made carvings in a script known as Rongorongo. It contains hundreds of shapes, many resembling plants and animals. No one has been able to decipher it. Each line was written in an alternate direction, starting in the bottom-left corner.

Moving statues

The *moai* were all carved in a quarry in the center of the island, and then moved several miles to the coast. How this was done remains a mystery. It was once thought that the islanders cut down their trees to make rollers. Experiments show that *moai* could have been "walked" upright, by rocking them from side to side with ropes.

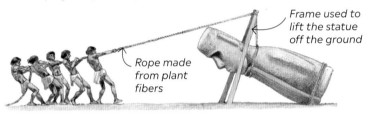

Frame used to lift the statue off the ground

Rope made from plant fibers

Raising a statue upright with ropes

Tangata Manu

Around 1500, the Rapa Nui began holding an annual contest where young men from each clan would swim to a nearby island to collect tern eggs. The clan chief of the winner became the *Tangata Manu* or "birdman" and would rule the island for a year.

Cape made from softened bark fibers

"Eyes" are made from carved white coral with a black obsidian "pupil."

The islanders

The Indigenous Rapa Nui people are Polynesian. Their native language, also called Rapa Nui, is spoken by around 1,000 people and is similar to other Polynesian languages, such as Hawaiian and Tahitian. The island's official language, though, is Spanish.

Restored statues

Some of the *moai* statues, which were all toppled, have now been restored. They have been set back on stone platforms called *ahu*, while wearing their red topknots. The *moai* shown here has been given new eyes.

Machu Picchu

An ancient stone citadel, now in ruins, Machu Picchu sits on top of a mountain in Peru. The name "Machu Picchu" comes from the Quechua word for "peak," after the two peaks that stand on each side of the citadel. Machu Picchu was once inhabited by the Inca civilization, but was abandoned after the Spanish invasion.

Machu Picchu is located in the Andes Mountains in Peru, near the ancient city of Cusco.

Up in the clouds

Machu Picchu is set high up on a ridge in the middle of a tropical forest. Many people visit the site by bus; others hike along the Inca Trail, a mountain path that used to connect the city to Cusco, the great Inca capital about 50 miles (80 km) away.

Stone blocks fit closely together

Earthquake-proof

Machu Picchu contains almost 200 buildings. To protect the structures from earthquakes, the Inca stonemasons used a special building technique. They used blocks of different shapes, carefully cutting the stones so they fitted together tightly like pieces in a jigsaw puzzle.

 EYEWITNESS

Pachacuti Inca Yupanqui

Machu Picchu was built for the Inca emperor Pachacuti Inca Yupanqui around 1450. He took over the throne of the small kingdom of Cusco in the Peruvian Andes in 1438, and soon laid the foundation for an empire by expanding the Inca state. His kingdom stretched from modern-day Ecuador to Chile.

Huayna Picchu, the highest point, is said to have been the high priest's home.

Gold image of Inti

Sun worship

The Inca people were polytheistic, which means they worshipped many gods. The most important god in their culture was the sun god Inti, known as the protector of the people and a source of light and warmth. Inti was especially important for the royal family, because the Inca people believed that their emperors were direct descendants of the sun god.

Machu Picchu's buildings are linked by
3,000 stone steps.

Why was it abandoned?

Machu Picchu was abandoned around 1550. During this time, the Inca were at war with Spanish invaders (above), and dying from diseases the Spanish had brought with them. Machu Picchu was not destroyed in this war; instead, its people appear to have simply left.

43

The Parthenon

A temple of the goddess Athena, the Parthenon stands on the rock of the Acropolis (high city) towering over Athens, Greece. According to legend, Athena, goddess of wisdom and crafts, gave her name to the city. Built from 447–432 BCE, the Parthenon is famous as the most beautiful Greek temple in the world.

The Parthenon is in Athens, the capital city of Greece.

Statue of Athena

The temple held a 39-ft-(12-m-) high statue of Athena, with ivory skin and clothing made of 220 lb (100 kg) of gold. This is a Roman marble copy of the lost statue.

Incredible temple

The Parthenon survived almost intact until 1687, when it was badly damaged during a war between Turkey and Venice. There was further damage in 1799, when the British Lord Elgin took many of the sculptures to London. Despite all this, the temple still stands today.

Marble temple

Designed by the architects Ictinus and Callicrates, the Parthenon was built with sparkling white marble, brought from Mount Pentelikon, 8 miles (13 km) northeast of Athens. It is the only Greek temple made entirely from marble. In most temples, marble was used only for sculptures.

Central hall, or cella, surrounded by solid walls

Even the roof tiles were made of marble

Sculptures of gods, showing the birth of Athena

A small room at the back was the treasury of Athens.

Athenians come to admire the temple and its statue of Athena.

Gold-and-ivory statue of Athena in the main hall (removed by the Romans in the 5th century CE)

Computer-generated cutaway model of the Parthenon as it stood in ancient Greece

Restoration

Since 1975, there has been ongoing work restoring the Parthenon. A team of architects, archaeologists, and engineers is taking all the marble fragments that lie scattered on the ground and replacing them on the temple walls. Where new marble is needed, it is brought from the original quarry on Mount Pentelikon.

Parthenon frieze

The Parthenon was richly decorated with sculptures, carved by the Athenian artist, Phidias. A long frieze running around the inner wall showed a religious procession of Athenians bringing offerings to the gods, seated at a feast. This was originally painted in bright colors.

The Parthenon has been used as a church, a mosque, and a weapons arsenal.

Petra

Petra is an ancient city in southern Jordan, halfway between the Dead Sea and the Red Sea.

Almost 2,000 years ago, Petra was a bustling desert city built by the Nabataeans, an ancient Arab people who were merchants and craftspeople. Today, all that remains of the city are massive structures carved into the cliffs. After 900 years as one of the world's wealthiest cities, changing trade routes led to Petra's decline.

Al-Dayr (The Monastery) is as tall as a modern five-story building.

Red sandstone cliffs

Sculpted in stone

The name "Petra" comes from the Greek word for "rock." The city's monuments are carved into the surrounding cliffs and the rooms inside it are hollowed-out caves. Petra is also called the "Rose city" because the sandstone rock-face into which it is built is pink and red in color.

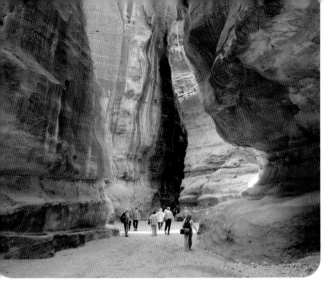

The mountain corridor

The main path leading to Petra is called the Siq, a narrow, winding, ¾-mile (1.2-km) gorge that cuts though the mountain. The Siq kept the city well-protected and very difficult to find. This explains why Petra remained undiscovered for many years.

Ornate pottery

It is thought that Petra was home to around 20,000 Nabataeans. Artifacts found in the city reveal that the people who lived here were highly skilled at making delicate plates and bowls for everyday use. Many items feature floral and geometric patterns.

Drinking bowl

Oil lamp

Caravan city

Merchants crossed the desert in caravans—convoys of camels laden with perfumes and spices. Petra was the crossing point of the routes between seaports and the cities of Damascus (in modern-day Syria) and Babylon (in modern-day Iraq).

Frankincense came from Yemen

Cinnamon came from Ethiopia

Cardamom came from India

City of tombs

Nabataean tombs were built high up in the cliff and looked like grand houses from the outside. Inscriptions on some of the tombs provide details about people who were once buried here, some of whom were Nabataean kings.

Graves in a Petra tomb

Sacred land

The Nabataeans originally worshipped many gods. However, from the beginning of the 4th century CE, the region came under the influence of Christianity, and then later Islam. According to Islamic tradition, Petra was built on the very spot where Moses—a prophet in Islam, Judaism, and Christianity—struck a rock, creating a stream of water to save his people from thirst. The valley's Arabic name is Wadi Musa, which means "valley of Moses."

A 17th-century painting illustrating the story of Moses bringing water to his people

Nabataean writing on clay tablet

Ancient script

The Nabataeans had their own alphabet with 22 letters, which later developed to become the Arabic alphabet. Like Arabic, it was written from right to left.

The Great Wall follows the top of the mountain ridg[e]

Watchtowers, from where guards looked out for invaders

The Ming Wall

Following its early construction, the Great Wall was added to and repaired many times over the centuries. Between the 3rd and 5th centuries CE, the Han and Jin dynasties extended the wall, while the Ming Dynasty (1368–1644 CE) built the long section of the wall that is visible today. The Ming Wall was mostly made of fired bricks. In places where they had no clay or fuel for bricks, they used stone, earth, or mud.

The Great Wall runs through northern China, all the way to the East China Sea.

The Great Wall of China

The world's largest human-made structure, the Great Wall of China is more than 12,400 miles (20,000 km) long. Its construction began in the 2nd century BCE, with further extensions added over the next 1,700 years. The wall features watchtowers and gatehouses, forming a strong defense system.

The first emperor

Until 221 BCE, China, previously divided into several warring states, was united by the ruler of Qin. He took on a new title, Qin Shi Huangdi, meaning "First Emperor of China." The emperor ordered the Great Wall to be built to mark the northern boundary of his empire.

Into the sea

The Laolongtou is the easternmost fortres[s] of the Great Wall where it meets the sea. It is als[o] called the Old Dragon Head, because it looks lik[e] a stone dragon drinking water from the sea[.]

Steps on the wall can be very steep and uneven.

Desert fort

The fortresses on the Great Wall, known as passes, are the only places that travelers can cross over. The Jiayuguan Fortress, in the Gobi Desert, protects the western end of the wall. In this desert region, the wall was made from rammed earth and dried mud bricks.

Helpful dragon

Chinese folklore regards dragons as kindly creatures that live in rivers and mountains. According to legend, a helpful dragon laid out the course of the wall across the landscape.

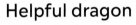

Copper statue of a Chinese dragon

Strong defense

The Great Wall was built as a defense against invaders. However, it could not keep out the fierce Mongols who lived to the north. In the 13th century, they crossed the wall and conquered the whole of China.

The wall today

Not all visitors to the Great Wall come to see the view. Every year, a marathon is hosted on the eastern section of the wall, near Beijing. Runners have to climb 5,164 steps during the race!

49

The Eiffel Tower

The Eiffel Tower is one of the most recognizable buildings in the world. Every year, almost 7 million visitors flock to the 1,063-ft- (324-m-) tall tower. On a clear day, visitors can see 37 miles (60 km) in every direction from the tower's upper level.

The Eiffel Tower is located on the south bank of the Seine River, in Paris, France.

The tower must be repainted every seven years.

Construction of the tower

It took 300 people more than two years to build the tower, which was completed in 1889. It is made of 18,038 steel components, held together with 2.5 million rivets. Each leg of the tower stands on its own supporting block, and the blocks are joined to each

Second level was completed in 13 months

Higher portion is painted lighter for a uniform effect

The third level is almost 900 ft (274 m) above the ground.

Radio transmissions

In 1903, a military radio station was set up at the top of the tower. It was later used to intercept enemy radio during World War I. Today, television and radio signals are broadcast from the tower.

The Eiffel Tower radio transmitter used in World War I

Tokyo Tower

There are replicas of the Eiffel Tower all around the world. Opened in 1958 and 30 ft (9 m) taller than the Eiffel Tower, the Tokyo Tower in Japan is painted orange and white so aircraft flying above can see it clearly.

Gustave Eiffel

The impressive tower design by French engineer Gustave Eiffel was chosen as the centerpiece for an international exhibition held in Paris in 1889. Eiffel had previously designed the interior supports of the Statue of Liberty in 1881.

*Philippe Petit
about to
complete
his stunt*

Balancing act

In 1989, French-born high-wire walker Philippe Petit celebrated the tower's 100th birthday by walking along a 2,300-ft- (700-m-) long tightrope from the Palais de Chaillot museum complex to the second level of the Eiffel Tower.

*The first level
is 187 ft (57 m)
above the ground.*

*... second level
is 376 ft (115 m)
above the ground.*

Towering over the skyline

The Eiffel Tower was the tallest building in the world for 41 years before New York's Chrysler Building was completed in 1930. It has viewing platforms for visitors on three levels, and restaurants on the first two.

To the top

Each level has a separate double-decker elevator to carry visitors. The Eiffel Tower has 1,710 steps in total, but visitors are only allowed to use the stairs up to the second level.

The pyramids of Giza

The three enormous pyramids of Giza are the burial site of three Egyptian rulers, or pharaohs. The tombs were built from millions of blocks of stone. The largest and oldest is the Great Pyramid. Its construction began around 2589 BCE and, at 482 ft (147 m) high, it held the record of the world's tallest building for more than 3,800 years.

Giza lies southeast of Cairo, Egypt, at the point where the desert meets the Nile valley.

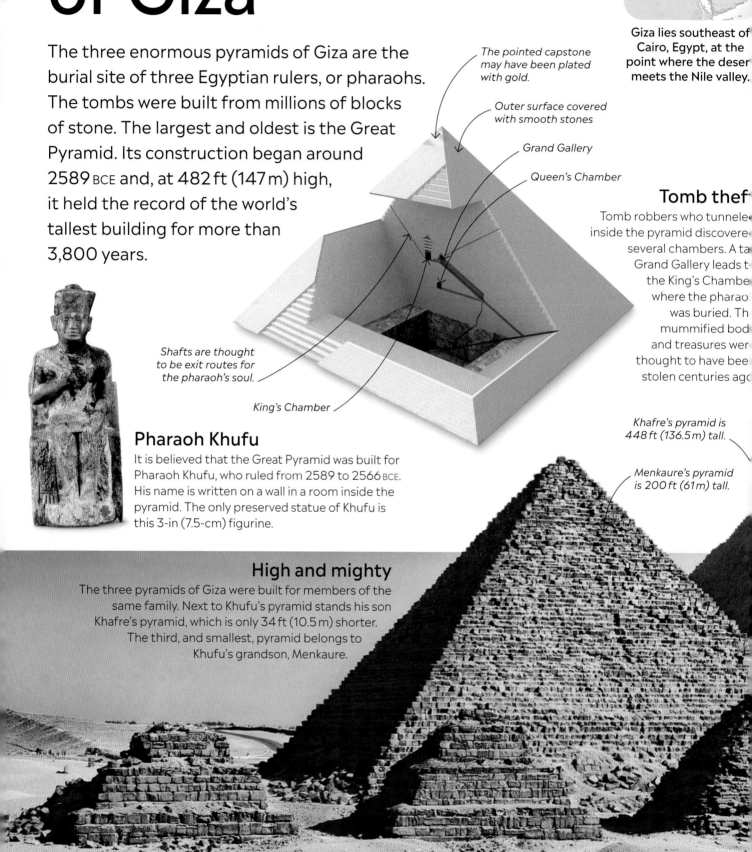

The pointed capstone may have been plated with gold.

Outer surface covered with smooth stones

Grand Gallery

Queen's Chamber

Shafts are thought to be exit routes for the pharaoh's soul.

King's Chamber

Tomb theft

Tomb robbers who tunneled inside the pyramid discovered several chambers. A tall Grand Gallery leads to the King's Chamber where the pharaoh was buried. The mummified body and treasures were thought to have been stolen centuries ago.

Khafre's pyramid is 448 ft (136.5 m) tall.

Menkaure's pyramid is 200 ft (61 m) tall.

Pharaoh Khufu

It is believed that the Great Pyramid was built for Pharaoh Khufu, who ruled from 2589 to 2566 BCE. His name is written on a wall in a room inside the pyramid. The only preserved statue of Khufu is this 3-in (7.5-cm) figurine.

High and mighty

The three pyramids of Giza were built for members of the same family. Next to Khufu's pyramid stands his son Khafre's pyramid, which is only 34 ft (10.5 m) shorter. The third, and smallest, pyramid belongs to Khufu's grandson, Menkaure.

👁 EYEWITNESS

Monica Hanna

Egyptologist Dr. Monica Hanna leads the Heritage Task Force, which works to protect archaeological sites in Egypt from thieves. Her campaigning helped recover stolen objects and led to better protection of ancient sites.

Building the pyramid

It is thought that the pyramids were built by hauling stones up huge earth ramps that ran around the outside. It would have taken tens of thousands of workers at least 10 years to complete one pyramid.

The Khufu ship is the world's oldest complete boat.

Khufu ship

In 1954, 1,224 wooden parts were found buried at the foot of the Great Pyramid. They were assembled into a 143-ft (43.6-m) boat known as the Khufu ship. It is likely that this boat was a part of Pharaoh Khufu's royal funeral.

Great Sphinx

Standing 1,700 ft (518 m) in front of Khafre's pyramid is the Great Sphinx, a statue of a creature with a lion's body and a human head. It is 241 ft (73.5 m) long and 66.3 ft (20.2 m) high, making it the world's largest statue carved from a single piece of stone.

Robot explorers

Small robots are used to explore the shafts that run through the pyramids. The Djedi robot has a flexible camera, a drill, and an ultrasound scanner. Its camera found mysterious doors at the top of the shafts.

Smooth limestone covering the top section still remains.

The Great Pyramid is made of 2.6 million limestone blocks.

The Colosseum

In the heart of the busy city of Rome, Italy, stands a 2,000-year-old round building, towering over its modern surroundings. The Colosseum—the world's largest amphitheater—was built as an entertainment venue for the Romans. This massive arena once hosted epic stage shows and intense gladiator battles.

The Colosseum is in Rome, the capital of Italy.

Grand venture

The construction of the Colosseum began in 72 CE during the reign of Emperor Vespasian, the first Roman ruler from the Flavian family. The theater was completed under the rule of Vespasian's son, Titus, in 80 CE.

Brick and concret core—exposed when the facing was removed

The structure

The Colosseum was built of bricks and concrete (a Roman invention), and a facing of fine, white limestone covered it. In the 5th century, after gladiator fights ended, it was used as a quarry for building materials for Rome. Much of the outer wall is now missing.

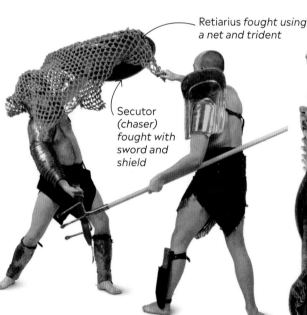

Retiarius fought using a net and trident

Secutor (chaser) fought with sword and shield

Gladiator games

Most gladiators were enslaved, prisoners of war, and convicted criminals. Sometimes, lower class citizens became gladiators to try for a chance at a better life. A gladiator who won a fight might be granted their freedom, and gain a cash prize. The emperor and crowd decided if the loser should be killed, or spared to fight again.

Inside the arena

An amphitheater is a circular, open-air arena surrounded by seats. The Colosseum could hold up to 87,000 people in three tiers. The hypogeum, a system of tunnels, ran beneath the amphitheater and was used to transport gladiators, performers, and animals to the arena.

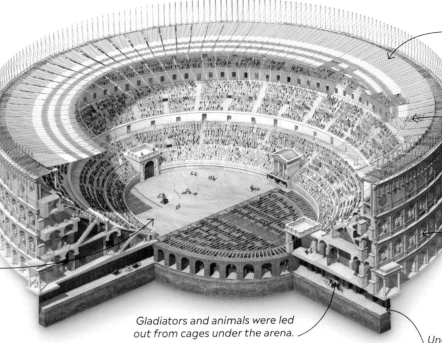

Sailcloth awnings shaded the crowd.

Women and enslaved people watched from the very top.

Outer walls displayed statues of famous Roman leaders.

Underground tunnels and rooms formed the hypogeum.

Gladiators and animals were led out from cages under the arena.

Wooden floor, covered with sand

Some helmets had a face visor for protection

Gladiator weapons

There were several types of gladiator, grouped according to the weapons and armor they used. Fights were usually set between different types of gladiator. *Retiarii* armed with a trident (fishing spear) and net always fought secutores—gladiators carrying a sword and shield.

Dagger, or pugio, used when the fighter had lost his main weapon

Unlike gladiators, bestiarii *did not* wear armor.

Leopards were common in Persia (modern-day Iran) in Roman times.

Mosaic depicting a gladiator battling a leopard

Animal hunts

Bestiarii (beast fighters) fought wild animals, such as crocodiles and tigers, from distant parts of the empire and lands beyond. For his games in 107 CE, Emperor Trajan brought 11,000 animals to Rome.

Flooded arena

In 80 CE, Titus filled the arena with water to reenact a famous naval battle. The floor of the building was waterproofed with canvas, and water was piped in until it was deep enough to carry full-sized warships.

Angkor Wat

Angkor Wat is located in northern Cambodia, near the city of Siem Reap.

The largest religious monument in the world, Angkor Wat was constructed during the reign of King Suryavarman II in the early 12th century. In Khmer, the language of Cambodia, "Angkor Wat" means "temple city."

Place of worship

Khmer kings, especially Suryavarman II, were devout worshippers of Vishnu, the supreme god in Hinduism. A shrine dedicated to Vishnu is located in the upper gallery of Angkor Wat's central tower.

Stone carvings

Angkor Wat's main building is enclosed by three concentric galleries. Its inner walls are covered in friezes (stone carvings) depicting stories of Hindu gods and heroes. The frieze called "Churning of the Sea of Milk" (left) measures more than 2,625 ft (800 m). It is said to be the longest frieze in the world.

Home of the gods

Angkor Wat was built in the shape of a lotus flower, an important symbol in Hinduism. The central tower represents the five-peaked Mount Meru, a mythical mountain believed to be the home of Lord Brahma, the Hindu god of creation.

Aligned with the sun

Angkor Wat lines up with the points of the compass, with the main entrance pointing west. During the spring and autumn equinox (the two days of the year when day and night are exactly the same length) the sun rises directly behind the central tower.

National symbol

n image of Angkor Wat appears in the center of the Cambodian flag. This magnificent temple has become a ational symbol of Cambodia's ancient Khmer heritage.

Rooted to the ground

The region around Angkor Wat contains many ancient temples and palaces. Many were abandoned, and the surrounding jungle grew around them—or, in the case of the Ta Prohm temple, on top of them.

Buddhism

About 50 years after Angkor Wat was completed, the Khmer converted to Buddhism. From then until today, Angkor Wat has been a Buddhist temple, except for a brief period in the 13th century when it was converted back to a Hindu temple.

Central tower, 213 ft (65 m) high

It took more than
30 years
to build Angkor Wat.

The **Taj Mahal**

Built in the 17th century, the Taj Mahal (meaning "crown of palaces" in Persian) is a beautiful example of Mughal architecture—a mixture of Indian, Arabic, and Persian styles. This white marble tomb is cube-shaped and looks the same from all sides. It is reflected in a long pool set in the center of the beautiful gardens.

The Taj Mahal is located beside the Yamuna River in Agra, in northern India.

Mumtaz Mahal

Mughal Empress Mumtaz Mahal advised her husband, Emperor Shah Jahan, on administrative matters, and accompanied him on his travels in his empire. In July 1631, she died while giving birth to her 14th child in Burhanpur, a city in central India.

The Mausoleum

The Taj Mahal was built in memory of the Mughal empress Mumtaz Mahal after her death. The richly decorated mausoleum (tomb building) is white, which stands for purity and is also a color of mourning in Islam. The whole structure represents the heavenly afterlife, with the bulbous dome representing the soul of the dead rising to paradise.

Internal decoration

The decorations inside the tomb are made from polished gemstones set into marble. Here, carnelian stones are used to make these red petals.

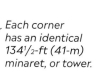

Each corner has an identical 134¹/₂-ft (41-m) minaret, or tower.

Royal tombs

In the ornate main chamber, two cenotaphs, or empty tombs, provide a memorial to Shah Jahan and his wife. Their actual graves lie in an undecorated underground vault, or burial chamber, that is closed to the public.

Persian influences

The design of the Taj Mahal was greatly influenced by that of the tomb of Humayun—Shah Jahan's great-grandfather and the second Mughal emperor. Built in Delhi in 1570, the red sandstone structure was the first example of a garden tomb—a Persian-style building that used symmetry.

The height of the dome matches the building's width.

Pishtaq, or archway

Lattice window

Each minaret of the tomb has the same chhatri, *or canopy, design.*

The lattice windows are made from sheets of marble with holes cut into them.

Plinth, or marble base

Writing on the wall

The Arabic writing on the walls of the Taj Mahal is taken from the Qur'an, the holy book of Islam. The words were written first on paper, then traced onto the stone before being chiseled out and filled with black marble.

Neuschwanstein Castle

Neuschwanstein Castle is located in the far southwest of Germany, in the foothills of the Alps.

With its ornate spires and tall towers, Neuschwanstein Castle looks like something out of a fairy tale. This lavish palace was built in the late 19th century as a luxury country retreat for Ludwig II, King of Bavaria. Designed to look like a medieval castle, it took about 18 years to build.

King Ludwig II

Glass painting

Although the castle was constructed using modern building techniques, it was decorated in a medieval style. The stained-glass windows in the king's bedroom depict his family's coats of arms. The blue-and-white checks are the symbol of Bavaria.

The monarch

Ludwig II invested in many grand projects and went into huge debt. His ministers wanted to replace him and had him declared insane. On June 12, 1886, Ludwig II was imprisoned, and the following day, he was found dead in a lake. It is thought that he may have been killed while trying to escape.

Room at the top

Built at the very top of the castle, the Throne Hall is one of only 15 rooms in the castle that were fully completed—the rest were never beautified. However, a throne was never installed in the room.

Swan King

Also known as the Swan King, Ludwig II modeled himself on the legend of Lohengrin—a knight who rescues a maiden on a boat pulled by a swan. The king filled his castle with decorations based on the swan. The castle's name, in fact, means "new swan stone."

Operatic inspiration

Ludwig loved the operas of German composer Richard Wagner, which were retellings of medieval legends. The castle's walls were covered with murals showing scenes from the composer's operas. Here, the mural reflects a scene from one of Wagner's operas, in which the warrior Siegfried kills a dragon named Fafnir.

The castle includes modern comforts such as heating, electric lighting, and telephones.

Paying tribute

Neuschwanstein Castle appears on the back of Germany's €2 coin. On completion in 1886, the castle was turned into a tourist attraction in an attempt to pay off its huge building costs.

Fairytale castle

With its soaring towers and grand staircases, Neuschwanstein Castle has become the inspiration for castles in many modern depictions of fairy tales. The Sleeping Beauty Castle, which opened in 1955 at Disneyland in California, was modeled on Neuschwanstein Castle.

Ludwig II lived in the gatehouse during the castle's construction.

Burj Khalifa

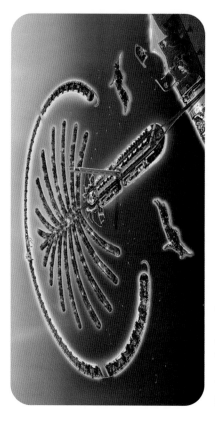

The Burj Khalifa is in Dubai in the United Arab Emirates (UAE).

At 2,717 ft (828 m) high, the Burj Khalifa is the world's tallest building. It took 7,500 workers 6 years to complete construction. Almost 121,250 tons of concrete—the weight of 100,000 elephants—and 42,990 tons (39,000 metric tons) of steel bars were used to build this tower.

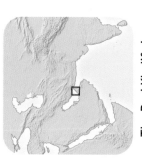

Spider lily

Desert flower

The architect Adrian Smith's design was inspired by the spider lily, a desert flower. The tower's three wings are based on the flower's petals. The wings get narrower with height, which makes the building very strong.

Top-down view

The central part of the building rises upward.

Wings narrow in 27 steps.

On the up

French climber Alain Robert took just six hours to scale the Burj Khalifa using only a rope and safety harness. In 2010, Nasr Al Niyadi and Omar Al Hegelan used a crane on the 160th floor to make the world's highest

Palm Islands

The Palm Islands are two artificial islands, each shaped like a palm tree. The coastline of one of the islands, the Palm Jumeirah, is 49 miles (78 km) long! Visitors can see these islands from the Burj's observation deck on the 124th floor, which also offers views of the Persian Gulf and the Arabian Desert.

STANDING AMONG GIANTS

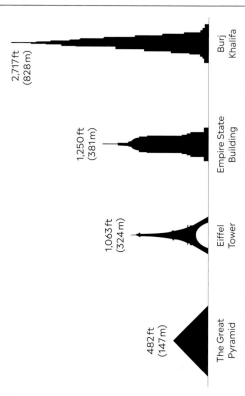

482 ft (147 m) — The Great Pyramid

1,063 ft (324 m) — Eiffel Tower

1,250 ft (381 m) — Empire State Building

2,717 ft (828 m) — Burj Khalifa

In 2010, the Burj Khalifa became the world's tallest building. The last building in the Middle East to hold this record was the Great Pyramid in Egypt (see pp.52–53), which held the title for more than 3,800 years.

Performing fountain

The Dubai Fountain, the largest "performing" water display in the world, is set in the artificial lake around the tower. It sprays 21,926 gallons (99,677 liters) of water 492 ft (150 m) high in the air.

A window cleaner hangs from ropes.

Window cleaning

Most of the tower's 24,348 windows are washed by automated machines. However, from floor 109 upward, they are cleaned by hand by a team of 36 specially trained window cleaners.

A special glass keeps out the desert heat.

Reaching new heights

The Burj Khalifa houses 1,000 apartments, offices, and hotel rooms. Although its elevator ride distance is the longest in the world, it takes only a minute to reach the top. The tower also features the world's highest restaurant (on the 122nd floor) and the highest swimming pool (on the 76th floor).

The Burj Khalifa has **163 floors** connected by 57 elevators.

The lower section houses a hotel.

Fireworks

The Burj Khalifa opened with a bang on January 4, 2010. The ceremony featured 10,000 fireworks and a laser light show. This was outdone on New Year's Eve 2013 by a six-minute display using more than 500,000 fireworks—the world's largest ever fireworks display.

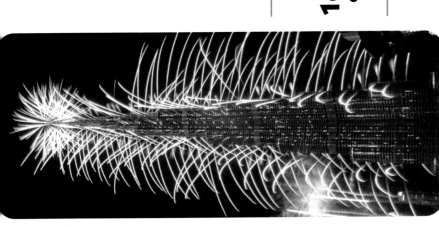

Ancient wonders

Ancient Greek travelers were the first people to create a list of the world's most amazing human-made structures—known today as the Seven Wonders of the Ancient World. Only one of these—the pyramids of Giza—still remains, while historical records tell us what the rest might have looked like.

Temple of Artemis

Built in 550 BCE near Ephesus on the coast of modern-day Turkey, the Temple of Artemis was dedicated to Artemis, the Greek goddess of hunting. It was rebuilt three times before it was finally destroyed by Christians around the beginning of the 5th century CE.

The third version of the temple had more than 127 columns.

Where in the world

Ancient Greek travelers could not travel all over the world, so the seven wonders were all in places they knew. Following the conquest of Alexander the Great, in 336–323 BCE, the Greek world included Egypt and Mesopotamia (modern-day Iraq), where Alexander made Babylon his capital

KEY ⬤ The ancient wonders are all near the Mediterranean Sea

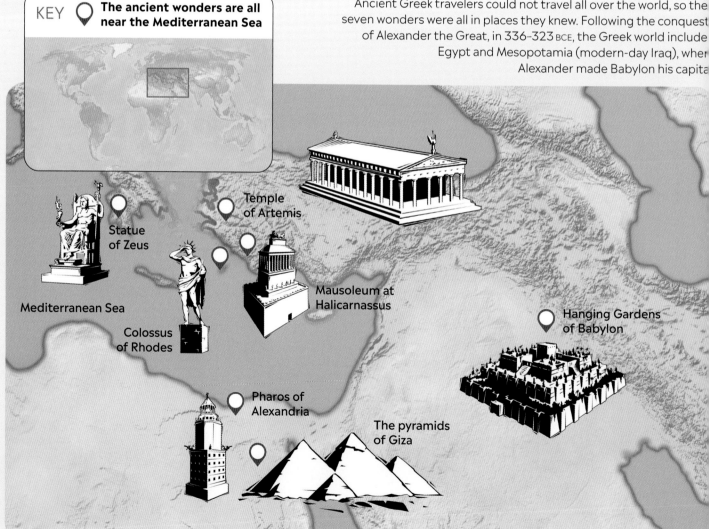

Statue of Zeus

Temple of Artemis

Mediterranean Sea

Colossus of Rhodes

Mausoleum at Halicarnassus

Hanging Gardens of Babylon

Pharos of Alexandria

The pyramids of Giza

Pyramids of Giza

The pyramids of Giza in Egypt were already ancient—around 2,000 years old—by the time Greek travelers wrote about them. Much of what we know of the pyramids comes from the writings of the ancient Greek historian Herodotus, who visited the tombs in the 5th century BCE.

Pharos of Alexandria

The world's largest lighthouse in ancient times, the Pharos of Alexandria was built in the 3rd century BCE and stood around 426 ft (130 m) high. It guided ships into the port of Alexandria, an Egyptian city founded by the Greek conqueror Alexander the Great. The building gradually collapsed after being damaged in three earthquakes, in 956 CE, 1303 CE, and 1323 CE.

Ships could sail safely by the light of the Pharos.

Hanging Gardens of Babylon

According to legend, King Nebuchadnezzar II of Babylon created the Hanging Gardens for his wife in around 600 BCE. The gardens had many levels, with exotic plants hanging from stepped terraces. Experts disagree about what the gardens looked like and whether they even existed!

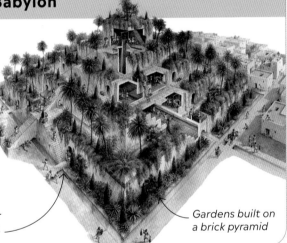

Channels brought water from the Euphrates River.

Gardens built on a brick pyramid

Colossus of Rhodes

This 20th-century painting depicts the bronze statue of the Greek sun god, Helios, that once stood in the ancient Greek city of Rhodes. Built in 292 BCE, the 147-ft (45-m) statue fell during an earthquake around 56 years later.

Crown of solar rays

Statue of Zeus

This 41-ft- (12.4-m-) tall ivory and gold statue of Zeus, king of the Greek gods, was built by the Greek sculptor Phidias in 435 BCE. It stood in Zeus's temple at Olympia, site of the ancient Olympic Games. It was destroyed by Christians in the 5th century CE.

The Zeus statue has skin of ivory, and clothing and hair of gold.

Mausoleum at Halicarnassus

In 350 BCE, Mausolus, the ruler of Caria in southwestern Turkey, built himself a giant 131-ft- (40-m-) tall tomb in the city of Halicarnassus (modern-day Bodrum, Turkey). The tomb became known as the Mausoleum. Its outer walls were decorated with statues of Mausolus and the gods, and carvings of battle scenes.

Record breakers

Various natural processes have combined to create some of the most spectacular scenery in the world—from giant caves and high mountains, to tall geysers and deep trenches. Today, people all over the globe travel great distances to visit these record-breaking natural wonders.

Longest river

Name: Nile River
Location: Africa
Length: 4,258 miles (6,853 km)

The Nile is the world's longest river, stretching north from East Africa to the Mediterranean. It flows through 10 countries in Africa, although most of it lies within Egypt and Sudan.

Tallest mountain

Name: Mauna Kea
Location: Hawaii
Height: 13,803 ft (4,207 m)

Mauna Kea is the world's tallest mountain from base to peak. Much of the volcano is under the sea, and so it does not rise as high above the ground as Mount Everest (see pp.6–7).

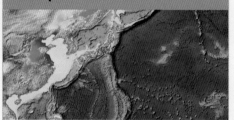

Deepest trench

Name: Mariana Trench
Location: Western Pacific Ocean
Maximum depth: 7 miles (11.03 km)

The Mariana Trench is the deepest place in the world. If Mount Everest were set inside it, there would still be around 1.2 miles (2 km) of water left above its peak.

Most active volcano

Name: Mount Kīlauea
Location: Hawaii
Last eruption: January 3, 1983–April 30, 2018

Mount Kīlauea is the world's most active volcano. Its last eruption lasted for 35 years, making it the longest ever recorded in the world.

Largest ocean

Name: Pacific Ocean
Location: From the Arctic to Antarctica
Area: 63,784,076 sq miles (165,200,000 sq km)

Covering almost one third of Earth's surface, the Pacific is the world's largest ocean. It is twice the size of the Atlantic, the second largest ocean.

Largest cave

Name: Són Đoòng Cave
Location: Vietnam
Maximum height: 656 ft (200 m)

Són Đoòng, the world's largest cave, is 5.6 miles (9 km) long and 492 ft (150 m) wide. In 2019, divers found an underwater tunnel linking it to another vast cave.

Largest forest

Name: Amazon Rainforest
Location: South America
Area: 2.3 million sq miles (6 million sq km)

The largest forest in the world, the Amazon has more than 12,000 species of trees. More than half of the Earth's plant and animal species live in the Amazon Rainforest.

Largest grassland

Name: Eurasian steppe
Location: From Hungary to China
Length: Around 5,000 miles
(8,000 km)

A vast plain running through Europe and Asia, the Eurasian steppe is the world's largest grassland. It is too dry for a forest to grow, but it gets enough rain for grasses and shrubs to thrive.

Largest ice shelf

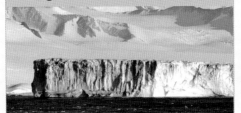

Name: Ross Ice Shelf
Location: Ross Sea, Antarctica
Area: 182,000 sq miles (472,000 sq km)

An ice shelf is a frozen sheet of fresh water, reaching from the coast into the ocean. The Ross Ice Shelf is the largest in the world (by area), and is more than 2,300 ft (700 m) thick in places.

Tallest active geyser

Name: Steamboat Geyser
Location: Yellowstone Park, Wyoming
Steam height: 300–400 ft (91–122 m)

The Steamboat Geyser is the world's tallest geyser. When it erupts, the steam reaches twice the height of Old Faithful (see pp.12–13). On eruption, it completely drains the underground Cistern Spring nearby.

Largest island

Name: Greenland
Location: Between Arctic and Atlantic Ocean
Area: 836,330 sq miles (2,166,086 sq km)

Greenland—the world's largest island—has more than 80 percent ice cover. If all the ice melted, the oceans would rise by 23 ft (7 m).

Largest desert

Name: Antarctic Desert
Location: Antarctica
Area: 5,339,573 sq miles (13,829,430 sq km)

A desert is a hot or cold area with little or no fresh liquid water. While the Sahara is the largest hot desert, Antarctica (made of solid ice) is the largest desert of all.

Highest tides

Name: Bay of Fundy
Location: Canada
Height of tides: Up to 53.4 ft (16.3 m)

The Bay of Fundy is in the Gulf of Maine in Canada. At high tide, this funnel-shaped gulf pushes rising water into the small bay, creating the world's highest tides.

Largest lake

Name: Lake Superior
Location: North America
Area: 31,820 sq miles (82,414 sq km)

The largest lake in the world (by area), Lake Superior is 350 miles (563 km) long and 160 miles (257 km) wide. The lake is famous for its crystal-clear water.

Highest waterfall

Name: Angel Falls
Location: Venezuela, South America
Height: 3,212 ft (979 m)

The Angel Falls is the highest uninterrupted waterfall in the world. It is 15 times higher than the famous Niagara Falls, which straddles Canada and the United States.

Longest fjord

Name: Scoresby Sund
Location: Greenland
Area: 14,700 sq miles (38,000 sq km)

A fjord is a long, narrow stretch of water surrounded by steep cliffs. Scoresby Sund, in the Greenland Sea, is the largest and longest system of fjords in the world.

Human-made wonders

Today's human-made wonders include huge skyscrapers of steel and glass, or vast tunnels, roads, and bridges that transform the landscape. These human-made wonders show us how technological skills have evolved over the centuries.

Tallest skyscraper

Although the United States was the first country to build skyscrapers in the 1880s, Asia is home to today's tallest buildings. Plans to build towers more than 3,280 ft (1,000 m) tall are currently underway.

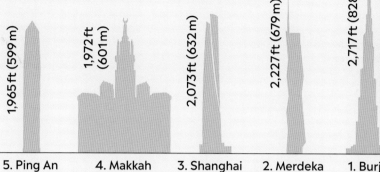

1,965 ft (599 m)	1,972 ft (601 m)	2,073 ft (632 m)	2,227 ft (679 m)	2,717 ft (828 m)
5. Ping An Finance Center, China	4. Makkah Royal Clock Tower, Saudi Arabia	3. Shanghai Tower, China	2. Merdeka PNB 118 (2022 completion), Malaysia	1. Burj Khalifa, UAE

Wonders in danger

Although most ancient buildings are protected by heritage organizations, many are still in danger of destruction. In the past, many sites were torn down so their materials could be reused in other buildings. Today's threats include wars, looting, climate change, modern development, and visitor numbers.

Most visited human-made wonders

Every year millions of tourists flock to see the wonders of the world. This graph shows the number of people who have visited some of these popular human-made wonders.

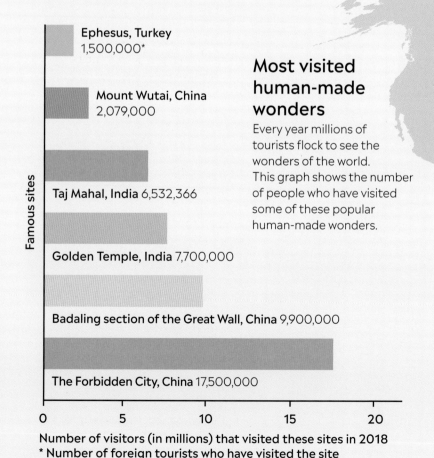

Famous sites

- Ephesus, Turkey 1,500,000*
- Mount Wutai, China 2,079,000
- Taj Mahal, India 6,532,366
- Golden Temple, India 7,700,000
- Badaling section of the Great Wall, China 9,900,000
- The Forbidden City, China 17,500,000

0 5 10 15 20

Number of visitors (in millions) that visited these sites in 2018
* Number of foreign tourists who have visited the site

Abu Mena Ruins, Egypt

Built in the 4th century CE, Abu Mena was a center for Christian pilgrims. Today, its ruins are in danger of being washed away by water channeled into the area for farming.

El Mirador, Guatemala

Discovered in 1926 in the jungles of Central America, this huge Mayan city dates back 2,500 years. The ancient city has been exposed to many threats, such as tree felling, looting, and road building.

Iconic statues of the world

Statues are built for many reasons—to celebrate the life of a person or an event, as art, or for worship. Shown here are some of the giant statues around the world as they stand today.

Christ the Redeemer, Brazil
125 ft (36 m)

The Motherland Calls, Russia
285 ft (87 m)

Statue of Liberty, US
305 ft (93 m)

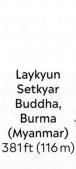

Laykyun Setkyar Buddha, Burma (Myanmar)
381 ft (116 m)

Chersonesus, Ukraine

The ancient Greeks set up a colony at Chersonesus in Crimea (modern-day Ukraine) 2,500 years ago. Today, the ruins are being torn down to make way for housing.

Bam, Iran

Built 2,600 years ago, the ancient fortress of Bam is the world's largest mud building. In 2003, it was badly damaged in an earthquake.

Old City of Jerusalem, Jerusalem

Built around the holy sites of Islam, Judaism, and Christianity, the city has been fought over by different religious communities for centuries. The ongoing conflict still threatens the Old City.

Kasubi Tombs, Uganda

The kings of the Buganda people—Uganda's largest ethnic group—are buried in thatched tombs, parts of which mysteriously burned down in 2010.

Engineering marvels

Roads, railroads, bridges, tunnels, and airports may often seem unremarkable. However, even the most ordinary-looking structures involve precision engineering. This makes the record-breaking examples all the more amazing.

Longest road
The Pan-American Highway in the US spans 30,000 miles (48,000 km).

Longest railroad
Russia's Trans-Siberian Railroad is the longest continuous railroad at 5,753 miles (9,259 km).

Largest airport
Saudi Arabia's King Fahd International Airport covers 301 sq miles (780 sq km).

Longest railroad tunnel
The Gotthard Base Tunnel in Switzerland stretches 35 1/2 miles (57.1 km).

Longest bridge
The Danyang-Kunshan Bridge in China, is 102.4 miles (164.8 km) long.

Longest road tunnel
The Lærdal Tunnel runs 15 miles (24.5 km) under Norway's mountains.

Glossary

AHU The platform on which the Rapa Nui (Easter Island) statues, or *moai*, were erected.

AMPHITHEATER An open-air theater, usually with the seats arranged in a circle or oval around a central arena.

ARTIFACT An object made by a human being, often of historical or cultural importance.

BACTERIA Microscopic organisms found in water, soil, air, and in and on plants and animals.

BAY An inlet of a sea or a lake that curves in toward land.

CANYON A deep valley formed when a river cuts through a mountain.

CAVERN A large cave. Caves form naturally due to rock erosion caused by water seeping through the ground. Caves can extend deep underground.

CENOTAPH An empty tomb used as a monument to someone whose remains are buried elsewhere.

CITADEL A fortress, usually on a hill, protecting a city.

CIVILIZATION An organized society in a particular area with a set way of life, culture, and language.

COLUMN A pillar that is used to hold up a roof, arch, or other parts of structures.

CORAL A marine animal, with stony skeletons, that can form colonies. These skeletons can build up to form coral reefs.

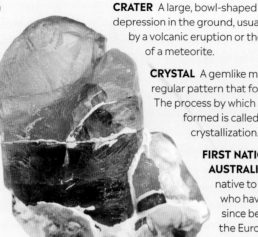

Olivine crystal

CRATER A large, bowl-shaped depression in the ground, usually caused by a volcanic eruption or the impact of a meteorite.

CRYSTAL A gemlike mineral with a regular pattern that forms naturally. The process by which a crystal is formed is called crystallization.

FIRST NATIONS AUSTRALIANS People native to Australia who have lived there since before the European settlers arrived.

FJORD A deep valley created by a glacier now flooded by the sea.

FORTRESS A heavily protected building, usually defended by an army.

FOSSIL The remains or impression of a living thing, usually preserved in rock.

FRIEZE A decorative carving running along the upper part of the wall of a building.

GEODE A mass of crystals that forms inside a space in a rock.

GEOGLYPH A pattern made on the ground using rocks, stones, trees, and soil.

GEYSER A natural spring that sprays boiling water and steam from the ground into the a[ir]

GLADIATOR A person in ancient Rome trained to fight against other people or wild animals in an arena, in front of an audience.

GORGE A deep, narrow valley, usually with steep cliffs on each side.

GRASSLANDS A large, open area covered in grass, with few trees.

HOMINID The group of animals that includes humans, along with chimpanzees and gorillas.

A lattice screen at the Taj Mahal, India

HYPOGEUM An underground complex, which usually has tunnels, dungeons, and chambers.

INDIGENOUS Someone who belongs to communities that have lived in a region for perhaps thousands of years.

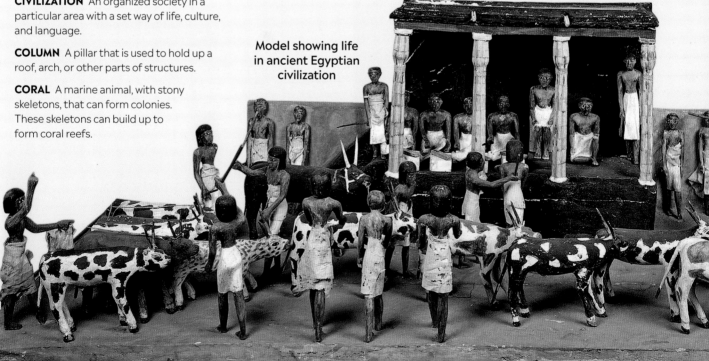

Model showing life in ancient Egyptian civilization

LATTICE An ornamental, netlike framework used to decorate buildings.

LAVA Molten rock that has erupted onto the surface from deep within Earth's crust.

MAGMA Molten rock formed deep within Earth.

MICROSCOPIC An object that is so small that it can only be seen through a microscope.

MIGRATION A journey, usually along a set route, in search of food and water. Animals migrate in response to changes in season.

MINARET A slender tower, usually part of a mosque (an Islamic place of worship), with a narrow balcony.

MINERAL A naturally occurring, solid substance that is inorganic (not made from the remains of plants and animals). Minerals cement together to form rocks.

MONASTERY A place where members of a religious community live and practice their religion.

MUMMY A body of a human or animal that has been preserved from decay.

MURAL A wall painting on dry plaster.

NOMAD A person without a permanent home, but who instead moves regularly.

OASIS An area in a desert where water is found.

OUTBACK The remote and usually uninhabited inland regions of Australia.

PHARAOH The title given to the rulers of ancient Egypt.

PLATEAU A wide, flat area of high land that rises above its surroundings.

POLYP An individual organism, part of a coral colony.

PREDATOR An animal that feeds by catching and eating other animals, known as prey.

The spider is a predator of the ladybug

QUARRY A place from which stone, rock, or other material is removed for use in building.

REEF A part of the seabed, often near land, and close to the surface of the water. It can be made of rock, or built up over centuries by corals that have hard, stony skeletons.

RIDGE A long, narrow hilltop or mountain range. It also refers to the top edge of a canyon.

Coral reef in Indonesia

SAFARI A journey taken to watch wild animals in their natural habitat.

SALT FLAT A large area of flat land, covered in a layer of salt.

SANDSTONE A rock made from ancient sand grains.

SAVANNA A dry grassland, where there is too little rainfall for forests to grow. Instead, fast-growing grasses cover the ground.

SHINTO A religion that originated in Japan, based on the worship of nature and one's ancestors.

SINKHOLES Holes that appear suddenly after rock and earth is washed away by water, and the ground collapses in on itself.

SPRING A place where underground water flows to the surface.

STEPPE A vast, flat area of land with few trees, especially in eastern Europe and Asia.

STRATOVOLCANO A cone-shaped volcano, with steep slopes, made of many layers of lava and ash.

TENTACLE A flexible, armlike limb of some animals, used for grasping, moving, or sensing.

TEPUI A word used by the Pemon people to refer to a type of flat-topped mountain found in South America.

TRENCH A deep, narrow ditch in the ground, often caused by the movement of Earth's crust.

VOLCANO An opening in Earth's crust through which magma, ash, and hot gases erupt; the structure created by the eruption is also called a volcano.

WATERING HOLE A pool in the ground from which animals regularly drink.

WETLAND An area of land covered with shallow water for large parts of the year. Lagoons, swamps, and marshes are all wetlands.

WOODLAND An area covered by trees.

Index

Acknowledgments

The publisher would like to thank the following people with their help with making the book:
Hazel Beynon, Esha Banerjee, Aman Kumar, and Sonam Mathur for text editing; Anis Sayyed and Govind Mittal for design assistance; Shelley Ware, Georgie Peters, and the DK London Diversity, Equity, and Inclusion team for authenticity checks; Saloni Singh for the jacket; Elizabeth Wise for the index; and Carron Brown for proofreading.

The publisher would like to thank the following for their kind permission to reproduce their images:
(Key: a-above; b-below/bottom; c-centre; f-far; l-left; r-right; t-top)

1 Corbis: 145 (c). **2 Alamy Stock Photo:** McPHOTO / vario images (tl); Sabena Jane Blackbird (cb). **Dorling Kindersley:** Hopi Learning Centre, Arizona (tr). **Dreamstime.com:** Engin Korkmaz (l); Neophuket (br). **Getty Images:** Lane Oatey / Blue Jean Images (t); Siede Preis / Photodisc (crb). **Robert Harding Picture Library:** Gonzalo Azumendi (c). **3 Dreamstime.com:** Witr (c). **4 123RF.com:** Raweewat Tuntisavee (tl). **Alamy Stock Photo:** Deco (br). **Dreamstime.com:** Luciano Mortula (br). **Getty Images:** DEA / G. NIMATALLAH (bl). **5 Getty Images / iStock:** Mlenny (br). **6 Getty Images:** Dmitry Pichugin (b). **Press Association Images:** AP (cla). **SuperStock:** imagebroker.net (c). **6-7 SuperStock:** imagebroker.net (c). **7 Corbis:** Stringer / Nepal / Reuters (cr). **Getty Images:** Jamie Marshall - Tribaleye Images / The Image Bank (tr). **8 Alamy Stock Photo:** Martin Harvey (b). **Robert Harding Picture Library:** Last Refuge (tl). **9 Alamy Stock Photo:** Flavio Varricchio / BrazilPhotos (tl). **Corbis:** Ch'ien Lee / Minden Pictures (clb). **FLPA:** Chien Lee / Minden Pictures (tr). **Matt Pycroft:** Coldhouse Collective / Berghaus (br). **PENGUIN and the Penguin logo are trademarks of Penguin Books Ltd:** The lost World by Doyle, Arthur Conan, 2007. Cover reproduced with permission from Penguin Books Ltd. **10 Dreamstime.com:** Thomas Humeau (bc). **10 Press Association Images:** Norikazu Tateishi / AP (tl). **11 Dreamstime.com:** Irina Drazowa-fischer (tr); Pondchao (tl). **Getty Images:** The Asahi Shimbun (cr). **Photoshot:** JTB (c). **12 Alamy Stock Photo:** eye35.pix (bl); Ron Niebrugge (tl). **12-13 Greg Willis:** (c). **13 123RF.com:** lorcel (br). **Corbis:** (tr). **Getty Images:** Stephanie Sawyer / Flickr (c). **14 Robert Harding Picture Library:** Richard Ashworth (cra). **Alamy Stock Photo:** Jack Sullivan (b). **15 Alamy Stock Photo:** Taylor S. Kennedy / National Geographic Image Collection (c). **Corbis:** Nathan Benn / Ottochrome (tr). **Ecole biblique:** © Photo Brown / Jerusalem (br). **Getty Images:** Ilan Shacham / Flickr Open (cla); Keren Su / The Image Bank (clb). **16 Dorling Kindersley:** Hopi Learning Centre, Arizona (tr). **Getty Images:** WIN-Initiative (c). **16-17 Corbis:** Kennan Ward (b). **17 Alamy Stock Photo:** NPS Photo (c); Robert Clay (b); joel zatz (t). **Press Association Images:** Tiffany Brown / AP (cr). **18 Alamy Stock Photo:** Bill Bachman (br); Michael Weber / imageBROKER (tl). **18-19 Dreamstime.com:** Matthew Weinel (c). **19 Fotolia:** Steve Lovegrove (tr). **Getty Images:** SAEED KHAN / AFP (tl). **20 Science Photo Library:** Javier Trueba / Msf (cra). **20-21 Getty Images:** Carsten Peter / Speleoresearch & Films / National Geographic (b). **21 Alamy Stock Photo:** Bill Bachman (cl); Nic Cleave Photography (cr). **Getty Images:** Carsten Peter / Speleoresearch & Films / National Geographic (tr); Siede Preis / Photodisc (c). **Science Photo Library:** Dirk Wiersma (br). **22 Alamy Stock Photo:** M&G Therin-Weise / age fotostock (br). **Corbis:** Kazuyoshi Nomachi (clb). **22-23 Getty Images:** Martin Child (c). **23 Corbis:** Atlantide Phototravel (br); George Steinmetz (t). **SuperStock:** Biosphoto (bl). **24 Alamy Stock Photo:** Sabena Jane Blackbird (clb). **SuperStock:** Biosphoto (c). **24-25 SuperStock:** Life on White / Purestock (c). **25 Alamy Stock Photo:** Ulrich Doering (clb). **Dreamstime.com:** Erichui (tr); Nolte Lourens (c). **26 Alamy Stock Photo:** McPHOTO / vario images (cl). **Dreamstime.com:** Luca Roggero (cl). **Photoshot:** Imagebrokers (b). **26-27 SuperStock:** age fotostock (c). **27 Corbis:** Theo Allofs / Minden Pictures (t); Peter Johnson (c). **28 Dreamstime.com:** Petrsalinger (t). **28-29 Getty Images:** Michael Nichols / National Geographic (b). **29 Alamy Stock Photo:** Christian Beier / CBpictures (tr). **Corbis:** Steven Vidler / Eurasia Press (cra). **naturepl.com:** Tim Laman (tc). **30 123RF.com:** Raweewat Tuntisavee (b). **Dreamstime.com:** Sburel (clb). **Robert Harding Picture Library:** Gonzalo Azumendi (c). **31 Dreamstime.com:** Bgminer (clb). **Getty Images:** David Doubilet / National Geographic (tr). **32 Alamy Stock Photo:** Paul Springett A (c). **Dreamstime.com:** Heather Rose (tr). **32-33 Alamy Stock Photo:** Thiago Trevisan (c). **33 Alamy Stock Photo:** David Wall (tl); Yvette Cardozo (bl). **Getty Images:** Stephane De Sakutin / AFP (tr). **34-35 Science Photo Library:** Philippe Psaila (t). **34 Corbis:** Caroline Blumberg / Epa (crb). **35 Getty Images:** Pierre Andrieu / AFP (b); Mira Oberman / AFP (c); Dea / G. Dagli Orti (tl). **36-37 Getty Images / iStock:** Nicolamargaret (c). **37 Alamy Stock Photo:** Adam Woolfitt / Robert Harding Picture Library Ltd (tr). **Corbis:** Richard T. Nowitz (ca). **Dreamstime.com:** Charlotte Leaper (tl). **Getty Images:** Image Hans Elbers / Flickr (clb); SOPA Images (br). **38 Robert Harding Picture Library:** Robert Frerck / Odyssey (cla). **Science Photo Library:** David Nunuk (cb). **38-39 Dreamstime.com:** Jarnogz (c). **39 Alamy Stock Photo:** Deco (tr). **Getty Images:** Dea / G. Dagli Orti (br).

40 SuperStock: Tips Images (bl). **41 Corbis:** James L. Amos (cr); Kelly-Mooney Photography (clb). **Getty Images:** Adrian Dennis / AFP (cb); Wojtek Buss / age fotostock (t). **Getty Images / iStock:** Mlenny (br). **4[?] Dreamstime.com:** Simone Pitrolo (cl). **The Bridgeman Art Library:** Brooklyn Museum of Art, New York, USA (crb). **42-43 Dreamstime.com:** Danilo Mongiello (c). **43 Alamy Stock Photo:** Deco (tr); Mireille Vautier (crb). **44-45 Getty Images:** George Pachantouris (c). **44 Getty Images:** DEA / G. NIMATALLAH (cla). **45 Alamy Stock Photo:** Classic Image (cr); Werner Forman Archive / Acropolis Museum, Athens / Heritage Images (clb). **46 Alamy Stock Photo:** F1online digitale Bildagentur GmbH (bl). **47 akg-images:** Jean-Louis Nou (br). **Alamy Stock Photo:** Hans P. Szyszka / Novarc Images (c); Coninch, Salomon de (1609-74) (attr. to) / The Art Gallery Collection (bl). **Getty Images:** Photodisc / Alex Cao (tc). **National Museum of Antiquities:** A. F. Voegelin, Antikenmuseum Basel und Sammlung Ludwig / Departme[nt] of Antiquities of Jordan (cl / Oil lamp). **Robert Harding Picture Library:** Andrea Innocenti / Cubo Images (cla). **48 Alamy Stock Photo:** The Art Archive (bl). **Getty Images:** Andrew Wong (crb). **48-49 Dreamstime.com:** Mauhorng (Background); Sofiaworld (t). **49 Alamy Stock Photo:** Liu Xiaoyang / China Images (cl). **Getty Images:** STR / AFP (br); Lane Oatey / Blue Jean Images (cr); Persian School / The Bridgeman Art Library (clb). **50 The Bridgeman Art Library:** CNAM, Conservatoire National des Arts et Metiers, Paris / Archives Charmet (tl). **Getty Images:** Bettmann (tr); photo by yasa / Flickr (cl); Nadar / The Bridgeman Art Library (tr); LL / Roger Viollet (cr). **50-51 Dreamstime.com:** Luciano Mortula (c). **51 Rex Features:** Sipa Press (tl). **SuperStock:** F1 ONLINE (b). **52 Getty Images:** Dea / A. Jemolo (cl). **52-53 Dreamstime.com:** Witr (b). **53 ©:** Monica Hanna (cla). **Corbis:** Aladin Abdel Naby / Reuters (cr). **Dreamstime.com:** Mahmoud Mahdy (tr). **54 Corbis:** Araldo de Luca (tl). **54-55 Corbis:** 145 (bc). **Dreamstime.com:** Mauhorng (Background). **Getty Images:** Dea / A. Dagli Orti (cl). **Dorling Kindersley:** Ermine Street Guard (cl / Military dagger). **Getty Images:** Dea / G. Dagli Orti (cl). **56 Dreamstime.com:** Noelbynature (c); Oscar Espinosa Villegas (tr). **56-57 Alamy:** Robert Harding Worl[d] Imagery (b). **57 Corbis:** Martin Puddy (cr). **Dreamstime.com:** Anil Grover (tr); Kjersti Joergensen (tl). **58 Alamy Stock Photo:** Dinodia Photos RM (clb). **58-59 Getty Images:** Gavin Hellier / Robert Harding World Imagery (b). **59 Dreamstime.com:** Shargaljut (cr). **60 Alamy Stock Photo:** Sergio Pitamitz (cr). **Corbis:** Adam Woolfitt (cb, bl). **Getty Images:** Dea / A. Dagli Orti (tl). **61 Alamy Stock Photo:** filmfoto (bl). **Corbis:** Markus Hanke / www.MarkusHanke.de (r). **Getty Images:** Dea / A. Dagli Orti (tl). **62-63 Dreamstime.com:** Engin Korkmaz (c). **62 Dreamstime.com:** Sippakorn Yamkasikorn (br). **Photoshot:** Al-Nakheel / Picture Alliance (tl). **Rex Features:** Sipa Press (br). **63 Getty Images:** Gilbert Agao (bc). **Getty Images:** Xu Jian / The Image Bank (cla). **64 Getty Images:** Print Collector / Hulton Archive (cr). **64-65 Dreamstime.com:** Lucasdm (Background). **65 Bridgeman Images:** © Look and Lear (tr); © Look and Learn (br). **Corbis:** Charles & Josette Lenars (tl). **Getty Images:** Culture Club / Hulton Archive (bl, bc). **66 Alamy Stock Photo:** Alvina Labsvirs (cb). **Dorling Kindersley:** Thomas Marent (br); Rough Guides (bl). **Dreamstime.com:** Dreamshot (tr). **Getty Images:** Toshi Sasaki / Stone (cr). **Science Photo Library:** NOAA (c). **66-67 Dreamstime.com:** Lucasdm (Background). **67 Dreamstime.com:** andreanita (tc). **Corbis:** Pete Oxford / Minden Pictures (cr). **Dreamstime.com:** Cosmopol (bc); Staphy (c); Josefhanus (cr); Paul Lemke (bl). **Getty Images:** Steve Allen / Digital Vision (r); GML / Flickr Open (tl). **PunchStock:** Digital Vision / Peter Adams (cl). **68 Dreamstime.com:** Ivan Sgualdini (br). **Robert Harding Picture Library:** Peter Langer / Insights (c). **68-69 Dreamstime.com:** Lucasdm (Background). **69 123RF.com:** Daniel Haller (tr). **Alamy Stock Photo:** Gustav Gonget / G[?] Images (bl). **Corbis:** Uwe Zucchi / dpa (tc). **Dorling Kindersley:** Rough Guides (cla, tc / Statue of Liberty). **Getty Images:** Carpe Fellner / Flickr (c). **Robert Harding Picture Library:** David Poole (cb); Eitan Simanor (cb / Bethesda pool). **70 Alamy Stock Photo:** Angelo Hornak (cr). **Getty Images:** Dea / A. Jemolo (b). **70-71 Dreamstime.com:** Lucasdm (Background). **71 Dreamstime.com:** Parnupong Norasethkamol (c). **Getty Images:** Blanchot Philippe / Hemis.fr (tr)

All other images © Dorling Kindersley
For further information see: www.dkimages.com